The Hymns of Shankara and the Wisdom of Advaita

Introduction

Introduction to the Philosophy of Advaita Vedanta

Advaita Vedanta is one of the most significant and influential philosophical schools of the Indian spiritual tradition. It is based on the concept of non-duality, which holds that the ultimate reality, called Brahman, is the only absolute truth, and that the phenomenal world and individuality are illusions. According to this philosophy, there is no separation between the individual and the universal reality; the Atman (individual soul) is essentially one with Brahman, the infinite and unchanging reality.

This vision has inspired millions throughout the centuries and has had a profound impact not only in India but also across the world. Adi Shankaracharya, one of the greatest sages and spiritual philosophers in history, was the principal architect of the dissemination and systematization of Advaita Vedanta. Through his teachings, he unified Vedic philosophy, resolved the apparent contradictions between sacred texts, and taught the path to realizing absolute truth through meditation, study, and discrimination between the real and the illusory.

The Purpose of This Book

This book aims to explore the life, works, and hymns of Adi Shankaracharya, offering a deep understanding of his philosophy and spiritual legacy. Through this journey, we will enter the heart of Shankaracharya's non-dual vision, seeking to reveal how his teachings can be applied in daily life to awaken the individual to their true nature, which is identical to Brahman.

The book focuses not only on his philosophical writings and teachings but also on the sacred hymns he composed. These hymns, which blend poetry and devotion, offer the reader a path of inner transformation, inviting deep meditation and realization of the Self. The hymns are presented as powerful tools for self-realization, and this work seeks to make them accessible and comprehensible through faithful translations from the original Sanskrit.

Why Read This Book

Reading this book is not merely an intellectual act, but a spiritual practice. Engaging with the life and writings of Adi Shankaracharya offers a unique opportunity to awaken the awareness of the unity of the Self with the absolute reality. Brahman is not an abstract concept but a truth that can be directly realized. This book will guide you on the path to that realization, using the words and teachings of one of India's greatest sages.

Each chapter is designed to introduce a fundamental principle of Shankaracharya's philosophy, starting with his most famous works and culminating in the interpretation of his hymns, which represent his highest poetic and spiritual expression. By the end of this book, you will not only have a theoretical understanding of his teachings but also a practical guide to integrate them into your everyday life.

CHAPTER 1: AN AGE OF ILLUSION AND THE NEED FOR AWAKENING

In today's world, where visibility, image, and appearance seem to dominate every aspect of our lives, the search for the true essence of who we are risks being lost in the fog of superficiality. We are often distracted by the pursuit of material success, the need for recognition, and the accumulation of wealth, while we forget that our deepest nature lies beyond all of this. Now more than ever, I feel within me the need to awaken the awareness of a reality that transcends everyday illusions—a reality that calls us to recognize the universal truth taught by Adi Shankaracharya through his philosophy of Advaita Vedanta.

The vision of Advaita Vedanta is not a denial of the world we live in, but a profound insight: the phenomenal world—of appearances and separations—is only a veil hiding the truth of oneness. It does not reject matter or sensory experience, but invites us to see beyond them—to realize that what is visible is merely a manifestation of something far greater, unchanging, and eternal.

Modern society constantly offers us distorted images of what is important: wealth, success, appearance. Everything seems built upon the illusion of separation—a constant play of opposites between self and other, between what we have and what we lack. But behind this mask, behind the veil of illusion (which Advaita Vedanta calls Maya), there is an absolute reality that connects us all. A truth we can recognize—if only we take the necessary step back, if only we cease identifying with the body, the mind, and the reality imposed upon us by the senses.

In a world that seems increasingly alienated from itself, where communication often appears to be a game of surfaces rather than substance, I believe it is vital to bring back into the light the teachings of those who have truly seen and lived this absolute truth. Adi Shankaracharya was one of the greatest sages who awakened humanity to the awareness of oneness. Through his writings, his teachings, and especially through his ability to unite Vedantic philosophy with devotional practice, he showed us the path to recognizing the truth hidden behind all things.

I am not speaking here of utopia or a mere hope for change, but of a radical awakening—a return to our essence. The realization of the Self is not something we can attain through external power or material possessions. It is a discovery that arises within us—an awakening that emerges when we stop identifying with what we are not and begin to embrace the deeper truth that unites us all.

The message of Adi Shankaracharya, through the Advaita Vedanta, is precisely that of going beyond the illusion of separation. He taught that Brahman, the absolute reality, is the only truth, and that the Atman, the individual soul, is one with it. The world we see and touch is nothing more than a reflection of that reality—a dream that appears real but is, in truth, transient.

At a time when we feel increasingly distant from our true essence, and the distractions of daily life cause us to forget what truly matters, the teachings of Shankaracharya offer a call to awareness. Not a call to inaction or escapism, but to the realization of a higher reality—one that enables us to live in harmony with ourselves, with others, and with the entire universe.

This is a declaration that what is within us transcends all appearances. A statement that all is One—that the separation between the individual and the universe is an illusion—and that the true meaning of life lies in recognizing and living this unity. Only then can we be truly free. Only then can we live in the fullest sense of the word—not as slaves to appearances, but as beings awakened to the ultimate truth.

CHAPTER 2: THE PHILOSOPHY OF ADVAITA VEDANTA

Advaita Vedanta is one of the most profound and influential philosophical schools India has ever produced. Taught by Adi Shankaracharya, it represents the path to the realization of the absolute truth. At its core lies the idea of non-duality. There is no separation between the individual and the universe. The central message that Adi Shankaracharya leaves us is that all is one. In reality, there is no distinction between what we perceive as "self" and what we perceive as "other." Separation is merely an illusion, created by the limited mind, which cannot see beyond the appearances of the phenomenal world.

Brahman and Atman: The One Reality

At the heart of Advaita Vedanta are the concepts of Brahman and Atman. Though they may appear distinct in words, Shankaracharya teaches that they are not separate realities but two aspects of the same essence.

Brahman is the ultimate reality: the absolute, the infinite, the eternal. It is the source from which all things arise and to which all things return. Brahman cannot be defined or confined by any word, concept, or attribute. It is not an individual or personal entity, but the universal principle that pervades all things in the cosmos. It is beyond time, space, and human imagination.

In this context, Atman refers to the individual self—but not in the conventional sense of a separate or limited ego. The Atman is the same essence of Brahman within each individual. When Shankaracharya declares "Atman is Brahman," he is revealing that our true nature is identical to the ultimate reality of the universe. We are not separate from it; we are not distinct from it. What we call "I" is actually the very essence of Brahman.

This concept stands in stark contrast to the view offered by the ordinary mind, which makes us believe that we are separate from the world, from others, and from the divine. Avidya, or ignorance, is the cause of this apparent separation. When we identify with the body and mind, we lose sight of our true nature, which is Brahman.

Non-Duality and the Vision of Oneness

The philosophy of Advaita Vedanta is grounded in a fundamental principle: there is no separation. Everything we perceive as separate, as autonomous entities, is an illusion produced by our limited perception. The phenomenal world, as we know it, is the result of Maya, the cosmic illusion that creates diversity and hides the underlying oneness. Maya conceals the true nature of reality, making us believe the material world and the distinctions between subject and object are real, when in truth, all is one.

This perception of separation, which we experience daily, is born of ignorance. Only when we transcend this illusion can we realize our unity with the whole. There is no "I" apart from the world; all is Brahman. The mind, the body, consciousness, the universe

—these are all manifestations of Brahman. Yet this unity is not immediately evident to us. Ignorance causes us to perceive a divide between the self and the universe, but once that veil is lifted, we can see and experience the truth: all is one.

The Phenomenal World: The Illusory Nature of Reality (Maya)

According to Adi Shankaracharya, the reality we see and experience each day is a manifestation of Maya, the cosmic illusion that creates the perception of separation between the individual and the ultimate truth. Maya leads us to believe that the material world is real, while in truth, the true reality is immutable and beyond form. The phenomenal world is transient, ever-changing, and impermanent. Brahman, on the other hand, is eternal, unchanging, and formless.

Maya gives rise to the illusion of duality: subject and object, the individual and the external world. What appears to us as separate and distinct is, in fact, a manifestation of one unified reality. Duality is the result of distorted perception. When we identify with our body and mind, we see the world as something external and separate—but this is only the effect of Maya. In reality, there is no separation. The phenomenal world, nature, other beings—they are all aspects of the one reality: Brahman.

Avidya: Ignorance and the Path of Knowledge

Avidya, or ignorance, is the root cause of our suffering and our separation from truth. Shankaracharya teaches that this ignorance is not merely a lack of intellectual knowledge, but a false understanding of reality. It is the illusion that makes us see the world as separate from us, that leads us to believe we are isolated individuals—when in fact, we are one with the whole.

The path to overcome this ignorance is jnana, direct knowledge. The realization of our true self, Atman, is the means by which we can experience the ultimate reality. This is not an intellectual exercise but a lived experience that allows us to transcend ignorance and see reality as it truly is: an indivisible unity where Atman is Brahman.

Conclusion: The Unity of Self and Universe

In summary, the philosophy of Advaita Vedanta teaches us that the separation we perceive between ourselves and the universe is only an illusion. Our true nature is Brahman, and there is no division between the self and the cosmos. Everything we see as separate is a manifestation of a single, indivisible reality. Ignorance leads us to perceive a divide that does not exist—and true realization comes when we move beyond that illusion and recognize our oneness with Brahman.

Advaita Vedanta is, ultimately, the path of liberation from separation, ignorance, and duality. It is an invitation to realize our authentic nature: that of totality. The awareness that all is one, that there is no separation between the individual and the universe, is the very heart of Advaita Vedanta.

CHAPTER 3: ADI SHANKARACHARYA – THE BIRTH OF THE MASTER OF ADVAITA VEDANTA

Adi Shankaracharya, one of the most eminent and influential figures in the history of Indian philosophy, is regarded as the founder of Advaita Vedanta—a school of thought that promotes non-duality, affirming that the individual Self (Atman) and the ultimate reality (Brahman) are one and the same. His life, spiritual journey, and writings have left an indelible mark on Indian spirituality and global philosophical thought. This chapter explores the origins, early years, and spiritual awakening of Adi Shankaracharya, his rise as a master, his philosophical battles, and his renunciation of the material world.

The Origins of Adi Shankaracharya

Adi Shankaracharya was born in the village of Kaladi, in present-day Kerala, southern India, around 788 CE. The legends surrounding his birth are as fascinating as they are mysterious and have contributed to the sacred aura surrounding his figure. He was born into a Brahmin family—priestly and scholarly by caste. His parents, Shivaguru and Aryamba, were devout worshippers of Shiva and prayed fervently for a child, as their marriage had been childless. It is said that Shankaracharya was conceived as a divine blessing after years of prayer and sacrifice, and that his birth itself was a miracle.

His childhood was marked by extraordinary signs. It is said that by the age of two, Shankaracharya could already recite and explain the Vedas, the foundational sacred texts of Hinduism that speak of universal principles and Self-knowledge. His life as a spiritual seeker and scholar was already taking shape—a prodigious mind with the innate ability to grasp complex truths, showing signs of a deep connection to universal knowledge and the divine.

His Encounter with Truth

At the age of just eight, Shankaracharya decided to embrace the path of renunciation and leave his family to pursue spiritual realization. But before taking this step, a pivotal event occurred: while bathing in a river, he was attacked by a crocodile. In that moment, sensing death near, he asked his mother for permission to become a monk, as he felt his spiritual purpose lay beyond the material world. Deeply moved by his conviction, his mother consented, and miraculously, the crocodile let him go.

This event—miraculous or symbolic—marked the beginning of his journey into Sannyasa, the renunciate life. He left home to walk the path of knowledge, meditation, and the quest for absolute truth. The young Shankaracharya embarked on the journey toward Self-realization, seeking to realize the Atman—the immortal essence that is identical to Brahman, the infinite and ultimate reality.

The Decisive Initiation and Meeting His Guru

Shankaracharya's spiritual path led him to meet his guru, Govindapada, a disciple of Gaudapada, the author of the Mandukya Karika, a foundational commentary on the Upanishads. Govindapada immediately recognized Shankaracharya's exceptional intellect and spiritual depth, and initiated him into the teachings of Advaita Vedanta—the non-dual philosophy that teaches the unity of the individual Self and the universal reality.

Govindapada instructed Shankaracharya in Jnana Yoga, the path of knowledge, guiding him toward direct realization of the Self. With his teacher's guidance, Shankaracharya fully embraced the view that only Self-knowledge leads to liberation (Moksha). The philosophical vision of Govindapada and the wisdom of Advaita Vedanta shaped Shankaracharya's destiny: to dedicate his life to spreading the message of non-duality.

The Path to Realization: Philosophical Struggles

Throughout his life, Shankaracharya was not only a student and practitioner of philosophy but also a renowned spiritual teacher and reformer of Vedantic tradition. His primary mission was to defend Advaita Vedanta against rival philosophical schools such as Dvaita Vedanta (dualism) and Vishishtadvaita Vedanta (qualified non-dualism). Shankaracharya became known for his skill in philosophical debate and his ability to refute schools that maintained the existence of multiple separate realities.

One of the most significant events in his life was his famous debate with Mandana Mishra, a prominent philosopher of the Mimamsa school. After days of discussion, Shankaracharya emerged victorious, converting Mandana Mishra to non-dual Vedanta and accepting him as a disciple. Mandana Mishra became known as Sureshwaracharya and played a vital role in spreading Advaita teachings.

Shankaracharya's works—including commentaries on the Upanishads, the Brahma Sutra, and the Bhagavad Gita, as well as treatises such as Vivekachudamani and Atma Bodha—are still studied today. He also composed devotional hymns that merged non-dual philosophy with bhakti (devotion). One example is the well-known Bhaja Govindam, which urges seekers to remember the Divine and not be misled by the illusions of the material world.

The Foundation of the Four Mathas

Shankaracharya established four major mathas (monastic centers) in India: in Sringeri (South), Puri (East), Dwaraka (West), and Badrinath (North). These centers represent the four Vedas and continue to uphold the Vedantic tradition. They served not only as schools of learning but also as spiritual hubs where the philosophy of Advaita was practiced through meditation and Self-realization.

His Death and Legacy

Shankaracharya passed away at the age of 32, but his life had a profound and lasting impact on Indian and global spirituality. The circumstances of his death remain mysterious; some traditions say he attained Mahasamadhi, the conscious and final renunciation of the physical body as a sign of ultimate realization. His early departure did not diminish his legacy—in fact, it amplified it. His thought and writings continued to shape the spiritual landscape for centuries.

His legacy lives on in the many schools of thought that derive from the Advaita Vedanta tradition, all of which honor him as one of its greatest masters. His philosophy continues to guide millions of seekers and thinkers, serving as a cornerstone of Vedantic spirituality.

Conclusion

The life of Adi Shankaracharya is an extraordinary example of how a realized master can transform humanity's understanding of reality. His philosophy of Advaita Vedanta, emphasizing the unity between the Self and the Absolute, continues to inspire and guide those who seek truth beyond the illusory appearances of the phenomenal world. The path he carved through time remains a beacon for those who walk the way of knowledge and Self-realization.

CHAPTER 4: THE GREAT TEACHINGS OF ADI SHANKARACHARYA

Introduction

Adi Shankaracharya, the master who systematized and disseminated Advaita Vedanta, left behind an extraordinary philosophical and spiritual legacy whose depth and relevance are still recognized around the world today. His works, teachings, and writings not only shaped Indian spirituality but also offered a path of realization that is universal—beyond any religion or tradition. In this chapter, we will explore the major teachings of Adi Shankaracharya, focusing on three key aspects: the Vivekachudamani and the importance of discrimination between the real and the unreal, his philosophy of unity, and his teachings on the Guru and the Path of Knowledge.

The Vivekachudamani and the Power of Discrimination

The Vivekachudamani (Crest-Jewel of Discrimination) is one of Adi Shankaracharya's most important works. It is considered his foundational treatise on spiritual discernment, known in Sanskrit as viveka. The text centers on the idea that the first essential step on the path to liberation (moksha) is the ability to discriminate between what is real and what is illusory.

In a world dominated by illusion (Maya), where the separation between the Self (Atman) and the Absolute (Brahman) appears to be real, Shankaracharya teaches that only authentic discernment can lead us to the recognition of our true nature. In the Vivekachudamani, he urges the spiritual seeker not to confuse what is transient and changing with what is eternal and unchanging. True discrimination, according to Shankaracharya, is not about judging external phenomena, but rather about seeing through the impermanence of physical reality and perceiving beyond the veil of appearances.

Shankaracharya emphasizes the importance of becoming aware of our impersonal identity and overcoming the ego, which binds us to the identification with the body and mind. The Vivekachudamani explores how ignorance (avidya) is the root cause of this misidentification. Discrimination between the real and the illusory is based on the understanding that Brahman is the only absolute reality, and all other forms of existence are mere projections of the mind. Through discrimination and detachment from illusion, the seeker can walk the path of liberation, recognizing that their true nature is already perfect and indestructible.

The Philosophy of Unity

The philosophy of Advaita Vedanta, as expounded by Adi Shankaracharya, is rooted in non-duality. The term Advaita literally means "non-dual," and it implies that there is no separation between Atman (the individual Self) and Brahman (the Absolute Reality). Shankaracharya strongly affirmed that the division between subject and object, between the individual and the world, is illusory—and that the true nature of the universe is oneness.

Throughout his works, Shankaracharya explained that Brahman is the only reality that truly exists—it is formless, nameless, and unlimited. Every phenomenon, every sensory experience, and even the individual self are temporary manifestations of this absolute reality. The experience of plurality, the division between self and other, is a projection of the mind that creates the illusion of separation—but in truth, this division does not exist on the level of absolute reality. Shankaracharya taught that once the seeker realizes the Self (Atman) as identical to Brahman, all distinctions between the individual and the universe dissolve, and one experiences union with the whole.

This teaching is encapsulated in the famous mahavakya "Tat Tvam Asi" ("You are That"), which Shankaracharya interpreted as the ultimate truth: the individual is identical to the Divine, to Brahman. The philosophy of unity is the essence of his teaching, which invites each person to see their essence as part of the whole, freeing themselves from all sense of separation and duality. Non-duality is not just a philosophical doctrine, but a direct experience of reality. Union with the Divine is already present in each human being, but our perception of this unity is obscured by the illusions of the phenomenal world.

Teachings on the Guru and the Path of Knowledge

Another fundamental aspect of Adi Shankaracharya's teaching is the role of the Guru on the spiritual path. For Shankaracharya, the Guru is not merely a teacher who transmits information or doctrine; the Guru is the channel through which direct knowledge of truth is received. The Guru represents the light that dispels the darkness of ignorance, illuminating the path to Self-realization.

Shankaracharya taught that true knowledge (Jnana) cannot be acquired through intellectual study or solitary contemplation—it must be transmitted by a realized master who embodies the direct experience of truth. The path of knowledge requires humility, devotion, and a mind that is ready to learn. Only the Guru, who has realized unity with Brahman, can guide the student through the process of Self-realization.

Shankaracharya emphasized the importance of non-verbal transmission of knowledge. The ultimate truth, which is beyond words and concepts, can only be perceived through a direct connection with the Guru. In this sense, the Guru does not simply convey teachings but imparts a living experience of truth. This spiritual connection is at the heart of all the Vedas and the Vedantic tradition, where the relationship between disciple and master is seen as a sacred journey toward Self-realization.

Shankaracharya invites us to seek an authentic Guru who can show us the path of knowledge and to follow their guidance with absolute trust and dedication. The true Guru is not only an external figure but also the inner master—the voice of wisdom that leads us through life's challenges. The relationship with the Guru is a path of deep inner transformation, where the disciple learns to transcend ignorance and recognize their own divine nature.

Conclusion

The great teachings of Adi Shankaracharya have influenced not only Vedantic philosophy but the entire landscape of Indian spirituality. The discrimination between the real and the unreal, the philosophy of unity, and the essential role of the Guru are the pillars upon which the Advaita Vedanta tradition stands. These principles remain vital for all those walking the spiritual path today, offering concrete guidance for transcending the illusion of separation and realizing our identity with the Divine.

The path of knowledge and realization is not an easy one, but the teachings of Shankaracharya invite us to walk it with clarity and courage—so that we may rediscover our divine nature and live in unity with the universe.

CHAPTER 5: DEVOTION AND THE HYMNS OF ADI SHANKARACHARYA

Introduction to Devotion in Advaita Vedanta

At the heart of Adi Shankaracharya's Advaita Vedanta philosophy lies not only an emphasis on knowledge (Jnana) and the discrimination between the real and the unreal, but also a profound recognition of the role of devotion (Bhakti) on the spiritual path. While Advaita is traditionally associated with the path of wisdom, Shankaracharya showed that devotion is not a separate or lesser path—it is complementary and synergistic.

His philosophy embraces an integrated approach to spirituality, where knowledge and devotion are not in conflict but converge into a single path that leads to Self-realization and liberation (moksha). This crucial aspect of his doctrine becomes especially evident in his hymns, which not only express devotion to the Divine but also serve as powerful instruments of spiritual realization.

The Role of Hymns in Advaita Vedanta Philosophy

Adi Shankaracharya's hymns are far more than poetic praises or ritualistic prayers to specific deities; they are profound spiritual tools designed to purify the mind, awaken inner awareness, and guide the individual toward realization of oneness with the Divine. Their function transcends mere adoration—they become a means for transforming consciousness and directly experiencing non-dual truth.

In his hymns, Shankaracharya masterfully blends Vedantic philosophy with a language that evokes pure devotion. Though Advaita speaks of Brahman—the formless, conceptless absolute reality—his hymns are crafted to awaken a deep emotional resonance with this truth. The non-dual vision of Shankaracharya is revealed in his hymns through the experience of unity, where the devotee is not separate from the object of their devotion, but is that very essence.

Thus, his hymns are not contradictory to his philosophical teachings—they complete them. While Vedantic instruction guides us to understand that our true nature is already perfect and one with Brahman, the hymns allow us to live that awareness, awakening the heart alongside the intellect. Devotion, in this context, is not external worship but inner purification, through which the mind becomes free of illusions and united with the ultimate reality.

The Role of Devotion on the Path of Knowledge

Shankaracharya never regarded devotion as separate from the quest for truth. On the contrary, he emphasized that devotion is essential in the process of Self-realization. Although knowledge is the primary means to overcome ignorance and attain liberation, devotion plays an equally important role. In his teachings, the Guru—the channel through which spiritual knowledge is transmitted—is seen not only as a beacon of light but also as the highest object of devotion.

In the Vivekachudamani and other works, Shankaracharya urges spiritual seekers to maintain a devotional and open mind, for it is only through deep connection with the Guru and the Divine that the path of realization can unfold. Love for the Divine and sincere devotion prepare the mind to receive ultimate truth. The path of knowledge is illuminated by the flame of devotion, for without it, the mind may remain closed, rigid, and unable to perceive reality.

In this sense, Shankaracharya's hymns are essential—not only do they cultivate the heart through devotion, but they also allow the practitioner to experience unity with the Divine. The repetition of his verses acts as a meditation that purifies the mind, preparing it for spiritual realization.

The Concept of Bhakti in Advaita Vedanta

Though Vedanta is primarily a philosophy of non-dual knowledge, Shankaracharya recognized Bhakti—devotion—as an essential aspect of spiritual practice. In the Advaitic tradition, Bhakti is not simply a feeling toward a particular deity, but a form of total surrender and unconditional love toward the Absolute.

Within Advaita Vedanta, Bhakti does not imply separation between devotee and Divine. According to Shankaracharya, Brahman is the only reality, and every act of devotion, every prayer, every gesture of love is, in truth, a recognition of our intrinsic unity with the universe and the Divine. Thus, Bhakti becomes a manifestation of universal love that reflects the non-dual truth of Shankaracharya's teaching.

In this way, Bhakti becomes the path through which the practitioner transcends the ego and recognizes that the object of devotion is not separate from the Self. Worship is not an external act, but an inner journey toward the realization that the devotee and the Divine are one and the same.

Shankaracharya's Hymns as Tools for Realization

Shankaracharya's hymns, such as the Bhaja Govindam, the Nirvana Shatakam, and the Saundarya Lahari, are expressions of Bhakti, but also serve as powerful tools for spiritual realization. With their sublime and potent language, these hymns express devotion while acting as vehicles for direct realization of truth.

Each word in these hymns is a vibration that awakens consciousness. Repetition of their verses has the power to purify the mind and lead to the awareness of the eternal Self. Bhaja Govindam, for instance, teaches us to detach from worldly illusions and reminds us that true peace lies only in the recognition of the Divine. Similarly, the Nirvana Shatakam articulates detachment from limited identities and guides us toward the realization that we are eternal consciousness itself.

These hymns invite us to see the Divine not as separate from ourselves, but as the very manifestation of our own essence. Thus, devotion is not an act of separation—it is a profound act of union with what already lives within us.

Conclusion

In conclusion, the hymns of Adi Shankaracharya are not only expressions of devotion but are powerful instruments for spiritual realization. His philosophy seamlessly integrates Bhakti and Jnana, uniting love and knowledge into a single path that leads to Self-realization. Though written as acts of devotion and reverence, his hymns function as spiritual practices that purify the mind and prepare the practitioner for direct perception of truth.

This integration of devotion and knowledge makes Shankaracharya's hymns a unique and potent means for accessing the ultimate truth. As the great master taught, love and knowledge are never separate: both lead to the realization of unity with the Divine.

CHAPTER 6: PHILOSOPHICAL WORKS OF ADI SHANKARACHARYA

1. Brahma Sutra Bhashya

One of the most significant and decisive works in the philosophy of Adi Shankaracharya is his Brahma Sutra Bhashya, a commentary on the Brahma Sutras, one of the principal texts of Vedanta, written by the sage Badarayana. This text is of fundamental importance for understanding Vedantic philosophy and serves as a cornerstone of the entire Indian philosophical system.

The Brahma Sutra is divided into four chapters and contains 555 sutras (aphorisms), offering a synthesis of Vedantic doctrines. Its primary aim is to teach how the phenomenal world relates to the ultimate reality, Brahman, and how the Atman, or Self, is inseparably linked to this reality.

Content and Significance of the Brahma Sutra Bhashya

Adi Shankaracharya's commentary stands out for its clear, incisive, and systematic approach. He demonstrates that the non-dualistic (Advaita) view is the key to understanding the Brahma Sutras and, consequently, the true nature of existence. His interpretation centers on the fundamental assertion that Atman (the individual Self) and Brahman (the Ultimate Reality) are one and the same. In other words, there is no separation between individuality and the Absolute. Duality is a mere illusion created by ignorance (avidya).

Key Principles of the Brahma Sutra Bhashya

1. The Unity of Atman and Brahman

One of Shankaracharya's most powerful assertions concerns non-duality: the Atman is not separate from Brahman. The individual awareness we think we possess is merely a projection of the Absolute, which is indivisible and all-pervading. The illusion of separation is the result of ignorance, but the true nature of the individual is the Absolute itself.

2. Maya (Illusion)

Shankaracharya emphasizes that the phenomenal world we perceive through the senses is an illusion (Maya). It is not that the world does not exist, but rather that the reality we perceive through the senses is not the ultimate truth. The ultimate truth can only be perceived through self-realization and deep meditation.

3. The Role of Knowledge (Jnana)

According to Shankaracharya, knowledge is the principal means to free oneself from ignorance and realize the unity between Atman and Brahman. In this context, true knowledge is not intellectual but a direct and experiential understanding of reality.

4. Liberation (Moksha)

Liberation, or Moksha, is not a change that occurs in the external world, but the inner realization that the individual is not separate from Brahman. It is the dissolution of duality and the awakening to the truth that all is One. Liberation is attained only when the individual recognizes their true nature as Brahman.

Insights and Interpretation of Shankaracharya's Commentary

The Brahma Sutra Bhashya is fundamental because it provides the philosophical foundation for understanding the doctrine of Advaita Vedanta. The commentary not only clarifies the concepts expressed in the original sutras but deepens them, applying philosophical thought to existential and spiritual questions.

One of Shankaracharya's key innovations is his interpretation of non-duality (Advaita), which not only rejects dualistic views but also offers a synthesis of metaphysics, theology, and spiritual practice. The unity of Atman and Brahman is not merely a philosophical abstraction but has practical implications for meditation and Self-realization.

Shankaracharya also addresses criticisms from other philosophical schools such as Samkhya and Nyaya, reaffirming that true understanding of Brahman can only come through direct experience, not through reasoning or scholastic logic. Vedantic philosophy is not a system of thought limited to abstract concepts, but a direct path toward the realization of the divine within oneself.

Conclusion of the Chapter

The Brahma Sutra Bhashya is one of the most powerful and influential works of Adi Shankaracharya, having had a profound impact on the Vedantic tradition. The commentary not only clarifies the meaning of the sutras but expands the understanding of non-duality and the unity of the Self with the Absolute. For those seeking a guide toward Self-realization, the Brahma Sutra Bhashya is a foundational work that continues to inspire and illuminate the minds of spiritual seekers.

In this chapter, we explored the central concepts of the Brahma

Sutra Bhashya and Shankaracharya's non-dualistic vision. Non-duality is not just a philosophical concept but a vivid experience that transforms one's perception of reality, guiding the individual toward final liberation, Self-realization, and union with the Divine.

CHAPTER 7: BHAGAVAD GITA BHASHYA

Introduction to the Bhagavad Gita Bhashya

One of the most significant texts in the Vedantic tradition is undoubtedly the Bhagavad Gita, one of the most sacred scriptures of India. It represents a philosophical and spiritual dialogue that has had a profound influence on Indian spirituality and philosophy. The Bhagavad Gita, composed within the epic Mahabharata, narrates the dialogue between Prince Arjuna and the god Krishna, who offers him guidance to understand his duty and realize the ultimate truth of reality. The Gita addresses universal themes such as karma, dharma, devotion, and knowledge, and represents a perfect synthesis of Vedantic philosophy.

The Bhagavad Gita Bhashya, Adi Shankaracharya's commentary on the Bhagavad Gita, is one of his most important writings. It offers a clear and incisive explanation of the Advaita Vedanta (non-dualism) perspective, which Shankaracharya champions, using the verses of the Gita to elucidate the philosophy of non-duality, where Atman (the Self) and Brahman (the Ultimate Reality) are one and the same, indivisible reality. In his commentary, Shankaracharya interprets every verse of the Bhagavad Gita through the lens of Advaita Vedanta, emphasizing the unity between the individual and the Absolute.

The Advaita Vedanta Vision in the Bhagavad Gita

The Bhagavad Gita unfolds at a moment of existential crisis for Arjuna, who finds himself facing a moral and spiritual battle. In this context, Krishna, as God incarnated in the form of a guru, imparts divine wisdom, explaining to Arjuna the meaning of various spiritual concepts. The Gita explores themes such as karma (action), dharma (duty), bhakti (devotion), and jnana (knowledge), but most importantly, it offers a profound vision of the unity between the individual and the divine.

Shankaracharya, in his commentary, clearly brings forth the non-duality embedded in the dialogue between Krishna and Arjuna. For Shankaracharya, interpreting the verses is not merely an intellectual exercise but a vivid realization of a truth that transcends words. The Bhagavad Gita is thus not just a philosophical text but a practical manual for realizing one's unity with Brahman.

1. Unity Between Atman and Brahman

The central theme of Shankaracharya's commentary on the Bhagavad Gita is the unity between Atman and Brahman. For Shankaracharya, the Atman (the individual self) is never separate from Brahman (the Absolute), and Self-realization means recognizing that there is no separation between the individual and ultimate reality. Awareness of the Self, according to Shankaracharya, is the key to understanding the truth of the world, of life, and of the divine.

A significant example of this vision is found in Gita verse 10.20, where Krishna declares: "I am the Atman residing in all beings." In this passage, Krishna does not merely identify with the universe or the gods, but clearly affirms his identity with the deepest Self of all beings. Shankaracharya interprets this verse as a confirmation of the unity of all things: Atman (the individual Self) is nothing but an expression of Brahman (the Ultimate Reality), and realizing this truth is the key to moksha (liberation).

2. Liberation Through Knowledge (Jnana Yoga)

In Shankaracharya's commentary, a central portion of the Gita is devoted to the concept of Jnana Yoga, or the path of knowledge, which is the means through which the individual can realize their unity with Brahman. The knowledge that leads to liberation is direct and experiential, not intellectual. This knowledge consists in realizing that Atman and Brahman are one single reality, and that the perception of separation is an illusion.

Shankaracharya emphasizes that while karma (action) and bhakti (devotion) are valid paths for the purification of heart and mind, it is knowledge (jnana) that is the direct means to dissolve avidya (ignorance) and realize the ultimate truth. In Gita verse 4.34, Krishna teaches that "only the one who has realized the Self" can attain liberation. Direct knowledge is the only path to comprehend the true nature of existence, which is non-dual.

3. The Role of the Guru in Transmitting Knowledge

Another fundamental theme in Shankaracharya's commentary is the importance of the Guru, or spiritual teacher, in transmitting knowledge. The relationship with the Guru is considered essential to follow the path to liberation. Krishna himself presents himself as Arjuna's Guru, imparting divine wisdom to help him overcome confusion and realize his inner truth.

Shankaracharya emphasizes that the true Guru is the one who guides the aspirant through the darkness of ignorance, offering the light of truth. The Guru is not merely an intellectual guide but a spiritual reference point who transmits truth without words, through example and direct influence. The true Guru is the one who helps the disciple realize that Atman and Brahman are the same reality.

4. The Importance of Devotion (Bhakti Yoga)

Although Shankaracharya's main focus in the Bhagavad Gita is on Jnana Yoga, the path of knowledge, he does not ignore the importance of Bhakti Yoga, the path of devotion. Shankaracharya recognizes that pure and sincere devotion to the divine is a powerful path that purifies the heart and prepares the disciple for Self-realization. Krishna himself affirms in the Gita that "whoever worships Me with faith reaches My abode."

However, for Shankaracharya, devotion must be accompanied by philosophical understanding. Bhakti without Jnana risks remaining a superficial practice, but when combined with knowledge, it leads to the realization of non-duality. In this sense, true devotion is not separate from the knowledge of the ultimate truth.

Conclusion

Adi Shankaracharya's Bhagavad Gita Bhashya is one of the most profound and significant works of Vedantic philosophy. His commentary not only provides a clear explanation of the text but also offers practical guidance for the spiritual path toward liberation. Advaita Vedanta, as explained by Shankaracharya, invites us to recognize that Atman and Brahman are one and the same reality, and that the perception of separation is an illusion.

The integration of Jnana (knowledge), Bhakti (devotion), and the role of the Guru as spiritual guide represent the fundamental pillars of the spiritual path toward truth. The Bhagavad Gita is not just a philosophical scripture but a practical manual that can guide every individual toward the realization of their true nature.

Shankaracharya's commentary on the Bhagavad Gita is thus a work of great value for anyone seeking to understand the deep principles of Advaita Vedanta and to embark on a journey of inner realization. Non-duality, as explained in the Gita, is not an abstract concept, but a living truth that can be experienced in daily life, leading to final liberation and union with the Divine.

CHAPTER 8: UPANISHAD BHASHYA

Introduction to the Upanishad Commentary

The Upanishads are among the most sacred and revered texts in the Vedantic tradition and represent the foundation of India's spiritual philosophy. These writings explore the nature of the universe, the ultimate truth, and the relationship between the individual and the Absolute. They offer a metaphysical vision that transcends Vedic rituals, focusing instead on the realization of the ultimate reality, Brahman, and the relationship between the Atman (the Self) and this transcendental truth. Over the centuries, the Upanishads have been interpreted in many ways, but Adi Shankaracharya's commentary stands among the most significant and influential. His work systematized and made accessible the fundamental principles of Advaita Vedanta.

In his Upanishad Bhashya (commentary on the Upanishads), Shankaracharya offers a non-dualistic reading of the sacred texts, providing a clear exposition of Vedantic thought, wherein Brahman is seen as the sole eternal and immutable reality, and everything that appears in the phenomenal world is a manifestation of that reality. In this chapter, we explore the key points of his commentary and how Shankaracharya interprets the major passages of the Upanishads through the lens of non-duality.

The Non-Dualistic Vision of the Upanishads

From their very origins, the Upanishads emphasize the centrality of the ultimate reality, Brahman, as the substance from which all emerges and to which all returns. However, traditional interpretations often portrayed Brahman as mysterious and distant—difficult for the ordinary individual to comprehend. Shankaracharya, through his commentary, helped clarify this concept by highlighting the non-dual nature of Brahman. According to him, the Atman (individual Self) and Brahman (ultimate reality) are one and the same, and the perception of separation is the result of ignorance (avidya).

The celebrated Upanishadic teaching Tat Tvam Asi ("Thou art That") affirms that the individual is not separate from Brahman, but is, in truth, a manifestation of it. This concept is central to Shankaracharya's thought, who in every interpretation emphasizes that the realization of ultimate truth is a process of self-revelation. There is no need to "find" Brahman outside; rather, it must be recognized as our intrinsic essence.

In his commentary on the Upanishads, Shankaracharya stresses that the duality we perceive in daily life—between subject and object, between Atman and Brahman—is illusory. The separation between the individual and the universe is caused by ignorance, and when this ignorance is dissolved through knowledge (jnana), the individual realizes their unity with Brahman. Ultimate reality is not separate from anything but is inherently present in every aspect of existence.

The Concept of Brahman in the Upanishads

In the Upanishad Bhashya, Shankaracharya offers a foundational interpretation of Brahman as the first cause and eternal reality. Brahman is described as the Absolute—without attributes, without form, and beyond intellectual comprehension. It is the only reality that truly exists, while everything we see and perceive through the senses is merely a temporary and illusory manifestation of Brahman.

One of the most powerful concepts Shankaracharya draws from the Upanishads is Sat-Cit-Ananda—"Being-Consciousness-Bliss." According to him, Brahman is the totality of existence, encompassing not only Being (Sat), but also Consciousness (Cit) and Bliss (Ananda). These three aspects are inseparable and constitute the intrinsic nature of Brahman. Our true essence, the Atman, is identical to Brahman, and the realization of this truth leads to moksha (liberation).

Shankaracharya interprets the Upanishads as direct affirmations of the non-dual reality of Brahman. In his commentaries, he explains that the words of the Upanishads must be grasped intuitively, rather than intellectually. The knowledge that leads to liberation is not acquired through information but through direct experience of truth. This experience is not something to be "achieved" in the conventional sense but is a revelation that occurs when ignorance dissolves and the individual recognizes their divine nature.

The Role of Ignorance (Avidya)

A central concept in Shankaracharya's commentary is that of avidya (ignorance), which is the primary cause of human suffering and the perception of separation. In Advaita Vedanta, ignorance is not simply a lack of intellectual knowledge, but a distortion of reality. Avidya causes the individual to perceive the multiplicity of the phenomenal world as separate from the Self, when in truth all is a manifestation of Brahman.

Shankaracharya insists that the path to liberation passes through the removal of avidya. Ignorance is like a mist that obscures our vision of reality, but when this mist is dispersed by the light of knowledge, the individual realizes that the separation between Self and the universe is an illusion. The realization of Brahman is thus a liberation from ignorance, and this process of self-revelation leads to direct experience of truth.

The Concept of Tat Tvam Asi

A fundamental element in Shankaracharya's commentary on the Upanishads is his interpretation of the renowned teaching Tat Tvam Asi, meaning "Thou art That." This statement, found in the Chandogya Upanishad, is one of the core pillars of Advaita Vedanta. Shankaracharya explains that this teaching is not merely a metaphorical assertion but a living truth that must be realized. The "That" refers to Brahman, the ultimate reality, and the "Thou" is the Atman, the individual Self. The realization that "Thou art That" is the understanding that the individual is not separate from divine reality but is intrinsically one with it.

Shankaracharya interprets this concept as the culmination of Vedantic philosophy: the recognition that there is no separation between the individual and the universe, between Atman and Brahman. Realizing this truth is the key to liberation from the cycle of birth and death (samsara) and the path to union with the Divine.

The Guru and the Path of Knowledge

Another essential theme in Shankaracharya's commentary on the Upanishads is the role of the Guru, or spiritual master, on the path to realization. He emphasizes that the knowledge of truth cannot be acquired merely through textual study but requires the guidance of an enlightened teacher. The Guru is the one who illumines the disciple—not only with verbal instruction but through the transmission of direct understanding of reality.

In his commentary, Shankaracharya highlights that the Guru is not just an intellectual instructor, but a living presence who brings the disciple into direct experience of truth. The relationship between Guru and disciple is central to the Vedantic tradition, and the Guru is seen as the bridge between ignorance and knowledge, between the phenomenal world and the ultimate reality.

Conclusion

Shankaracharya's commentary on the Upanishads is one of the foundational works of Advaita Vedanta. Through this commentary, he systematized and made Vedantic thought accessible, turning the Upanishads into a practical guide for those seeking to understand the true nature of existence. The non-dualistic vision that emerges from this commentary is not merely a philosophical theory but a direct experience of reality that can be lived through Self-realization.

Shankaracharya teaches that liberation is not a goal achieved through external actions or rituals, but through inner knowledge, the removal of ignorance, and the realization that the individual and the Divine are one and the same. His interpretation of the Upanishads is thus an invitation to look within and recognize our identity with Brahman, the one eternal and unchanging reality.

Chapter9: Vivekachudamani (The Crest-Jewel of Discrimination)

Introduction to the Vivekachudamani

The Vivekachudamani (The Crest-Jewel of Discrimination) is one of the most celebrated and foundational treatises written by Adi Shankaracharya. It is a text that combines philosophy and poetry, and its poetic structure makes it easily memorable, rendering its teachings more accessible. This treatise is not merely an intellectual work—it is a practical spiritual guide that leads the reader toward the realization of the ultimate truth. The Vivekachudamani serves as a manual for those who aspire to liberation (moksha) and provides the necessary viveka (discrimination) to distinguish what is real from what is illusory, the eternal from the ephemeral.

According to Shankaracharya, discrimination is not merely a mental distinction but a spiritual skill that leads to a direct understanding of reality. The discrimination between the real and the unreal is the first step on the path to Self-realization, and Shankaracharya teaches how to cultivate it through self-observation and deep reflection. This text is therefore essential for understanding the philosophy of Advaita Vedanta and for embarking on the path toward Self-awareness.

The Concept of Discrimination (Viveka)

In the Vivekachudamani, discrimination (viveka) is described as the capacity to discern what is eternal and unchanging (Brahman) from what is temporary and illusory (Maya). Shankaracharya teaches that the root cause of suffering and ignorance is our tendency to identify the Self with the body, the mind, and the phenomenal world—all of which are subject to change and death. Discrimination involves the ability to see beyond appearances and recognize that what truly belongs to us is not the body nor the mind, but the Atman—the eternal Self—which is identical to Brahman.

According to Shankaracharya, only through this discrimination can we free the mind from illusions and discover our true nature. The Vivekachudamani explores in detail how to develop this capacity, inviting the reader to reflect on their own identity and question the false beliefs that bind us to the phenomenal world.

The Path to Realization

The Vivekachudamani does not merely define discrimination but offers a step-by-step guide on how to cultivate it. Shankaracharya begins the treatise with a clear description of humanity and its flaws: attachment to material things, mental confusion, and fear of death. However, he affirms that through discrimination, these obstacles can be overcome. Self-realization does not require external actions, but rather a profound inner transformation in the way one perceives oneself and the world.

A crucial point in the Vivekachudamani is the reflection on the impermanence of life and the illusions it creates. Shankaracharya emphasizes that the world we perceive through the senses is only a manifestation of Maya, the illusion, and that only through knowledge (jnana) can we see beyond it. This is not a process that happens instantly, but a continuous journey of self-discovery and introspection.

The Three Pillars of the Spiritual Path

In the Vivekachudamani, Shankaracharya describes three essential pillars of the spiritual path:

1. Detachment (Vairagya)

This is the first step toward realization. It means renouncing worldly desires and attachments that keep us bound to the cycle of birth and death (samsara). Detachment does not mean rejecting the world, but rather freeing oneself from the bondage of desires and illusions.

2. The Path of Knowledge (Jnana Yoga)

The second pillar is knowledge, which Shankaracharya considers the only way to free oneself from ignorance (avidya). This knowledge is not intellectual but a direct experience of the truth. The practice of Jnana Yoga involves inner inquiry to discover the nature of the Self and the ultimate reality of Brahman.

3. The Path of Action (Karma Yoga)

The third pillar is selfless action. Shankaracharya teaches that in order to progress on the spiritual path, one must act without attachment to the fruits of action. This purifies the mind and draws the seeker closer to spiritual realization.

These three pillars are intimately interconnected and, for Shankaracharya, are all necessary for attaining liberation. Without detachment from desires, without knowledge of the Self, and without selfless action, one cannot advance on the path of liberation.

The Role of the Guru

The Guru plays a central role in the Vivekachudamani. According to Shankaracharya, the Guru is the one who guides the disciple in the search for truth. The master is not just a teacher but a living presence who transmits knowledge directly to the soul of the disciple. Realization of the truth thus occurs through the spiritual influence of the Guru, who reveals to the disciple their true nature. Without a Guru, it is difficult for the individual to free themselves from mental confusion and ignorance.

Shankaracharya teaches that the Guru is essential for unveiling the truth that is already within us. The relationship between Guru and disciple is fundamental for the purification of the mind and the realization of the ultimate truth.

The Meaning of "Tat Tvam Asi"

A central theme in the Vivekachudamani is the teaching Tat Tvam Asi, meaning "Thou art That." This statement, found in the Upanishads, is one of the pillars of Advaita Vedanta and is revisited and explained by Shankaracharya. "Thou art That" means that the Atman, the individual Self, is identical to Brahman, the Absolute. The separation between the individual and ultimate reality is an illusion born of ignorance. Realizing that "Thou art That" marks the culmination of the spiritual path, for it is the moment when the individual recognizes their unity with the Divine.

Inner Work: Meditation

Meditation is another essential tool in the Vivekachudamani for attaining discrimination and Self-realization. Shankaracharya emphasizes the importance of silent contemplation and reflection on the Self, as meditation allows the seeker to detach from worldly thoughts and perceive reality beyond illusions. Meditation on the mantra and repetition of the divine name (japa) are practices that purify the mind and lead to realization.

Conclusion

Adi Shankaracharya's Vivekachudamani is an essential guide for anyone wishing to undertake the path to liberation. Through this text, Shankaracharya offers not only profound philosophy but also practical spiritual guidance to help the reader cultivate the discrimination between the real and the unreal. The path to Self-realization, according to Shankaracharya, is one of detachment, knowledge, and selfless action, guided by the teaching of the Guru. The Vivekachudamani is not merely a philosophical treatise but a living practice that, if followed with sincerity, leads the individual to the realization of their true nature—which is identical to Brahman, the Absolute.

Shankaracharya reminds us that liberation is not a goal to be reached in the future, but a reality already present within us. Discrimination between the real and the unreal allows us to see beyond appearances and recognize our oneness with the Infinite.

CHAPTER 10: ATMA BODHA (SELF-KNOWLEDGE)

Introduction to the Atma Bodha

Atma Bodha is one of the most concise and significant works by Adi Shankaracharya, in which he explores the fundamental concept of awareness of the Self (Atman) and offers a clear explanation of the nature of ultimate reality. Though relatively brief, this treatise carries dense philosophical weight and is essential for understanding Shankaracharya's non-dualistic vision and the path to spiritual realization. In Atma Bodha, Shankaracharya clearly distinguishes between the illusion of the phenomenal world (Maya) and the ultimate truth, which is the Atman—the immortal essence that is identical to Brahman.

The work is composed in verse form yet remains extremely practical in its approach. It serves as a direct guide for those seeking to awaken their awareness of the Self, separating deceptive appearances from eternal reality. Like all of

Shankaracharya's works, Atma Bodha is not merely an intellectual treatise, but an invitation to live philosophy as a direct and transformative experience.

The Concept of Atman: The Nature of the Self

In Atma Bodha, Shankaracharya begins by clearly defining Atman, the Self. Atman is the eternal, indivisible, and immutable essence of every living being and is the source of all creation. The key distinction made in this work is between the Atman (the Self) and the body, mind, and emotions, which are all temporary and subject to change. The Self is never subject to death or destruction, as it transcends all transient manifestations.

According to Shankaracharya, the phenomenal world we perceive through the senses is not ultimate reality, but a projection of the illusion known as Maya. This illusion causes us to identify with body and mind, forgetting our transcendent nature. The path of Self-awareness, therefore, is a process of detaching from this false identification to rediscover our unity with the Atman and, by extension, with Brahman—the absolute reality.

Maya and the Illusion of the Phenomenal World

A central part of Atma Bodha addresses the distinction between truth and illusion. Shankaracharya explains that the illusion of Maya is the root cause of our ignorance (avidya). The world we inhabit, made of material objects, relationships, and sensory experiences, is misleading because all of it is destined to change and vanish. This world is apparent, not real, and our identification with it binds us to the cycle of samsara—birth, death, and rebirth.

Maya makes the world appear as though it were separate, when in fact all is united in Brahman, the Absolute. Liberation (moksha) comes through the realization of the true nature of the Self, freeing oneself from the deception of Maya. Awareness of the Self enables one to see beyond surface appearances and recognize that everything that exists is merely a manifestation of that one truth, which is Brahman.

Shankaracharya uses the well-known metaphor of "the snake in the rope" to explain how Maya distorts reality. Imagine mistaking a rope for a snake—our mind misperceives the world through Maya, seeing separation and difference where in fact everything is one. Spiritual practice and discernment allow us to dissolve this illusion.

Self-Knowledge as Liberation

One of the central assertions of Atma Bodha is that Self-knowledge is the path to liberation. Shankaracharya teaches that only through direct knowledge (jnana) can we transcend our sense of being separate identities and recognize our true nature. Knowledge here is not just intellectual understanding, but a direct experience that engages one's entire being. Through realization of the Self, we attain eternal peace, beyond the suffering and pain of the phenomenal world.

In Atma Bodha, Shankaracharya emphasizes that Self-awareness is not attained through external rituals or sacrifices, but through inner contemplation. The mind must be purified and disciplined, and the heart must open to the truth that dwells within us. The realization of the Self is the discovery that our true being is identical to Brahman, which is all-pervading, eternal, and formless.

The Role of Meditation and Spiritual Practice

Shankaracharya also highlights the importance of meditation on the path to Self-awareness. Meditation is a fundamental tool for concentrating the mind and turning attention away from the distractions of the external world. By meditating on the Self, the seeker can awaken to their divine nature and dissolve the ties of illusion. The repetition of sacred mantras (japa) is a common practice in Advaita Vedanta that helps focus the mind on truth and detach from mental and emotional attachments.

He emphasizes that Self-realization is not a one-time event, but a gradual process requiring sustained effort. The practitioner must purify the heart and mind, renounce illusions, and look within to discover truth. Constant introspection is what leads to the understanding of non-duality and the realization of unity with Brahman.

The Concept of Avidya and Direct Knowledge

Another core theme of Atma Bodha is avidya, or ignorance, which causes our separation from truth. Avidya leads us to believe that the material world is real and urges us to identify our Self with body and mind. This deception creates the cycle of birth, death, and suffering (samsara), which can only be broken through direct knowledge.

Shankaracharya explains that ignorance can be removed only by direct realization of the Self. Self-knowledge is not the accumulation of information, but an inner transformation that dissolves the sense of separation between self and the universe. The truth we discover is that we have never been separate from Brahman—we are, in fact, one with the Absolute reality.

The Path of Liberation (Moksha)

The realization that Atman is identical to Brahman is the path to liberation (moksha). Shankaracharya teaches that liberation is not a place or state to be reached in the future, but a recognition already present within us. Realization of the Self brings an end to suffering and eternal peace, as there are no more illusions to overcome. Liberation is the return to our original nature, which is infinite, formless, and without limitation.

In Atma Bodha, Shankaracharya guides us along this path, providing the tools needed to overcome ignorance and reach ultimate truth. This work is not just a philosophical treatise, but a living practice that invites us to directly experience the reality of our being, to go beyond appearances, and to discover our identity with the Divine.

Conclusion

Adi Shankaracharya's Atma Bodha is a text that synthesizes the foundations of Advaita Vedanta philosophy and offers practical guidance for those seeking to realize the truth of the Self. Discriminating between what is real and what is illusory is the first step to freeing ourselves from the chains of ignorance and recognizing our unity with Brahman. Through meditation, reflection, and introspection, we can experience the truth that resides within and attain liberation.

Shankaracharya reminds us that the realization of the Self is the realization of Brahman, and that suffering, attachment, and illusion are only temporary. The path of knowledge is the path to eternal peace, and the ultimate truth is this: we are already that which we seek.

CHAPTER 11: ADHYATMA VIDYA (SPIRITUAL KNOWLEDGE)

Introduction to Adhyatma Vidya

Adhyatma Vidya, which translates as "Spiritual Knowledge," is one of Adi Shankaracharya's philosophical works that deeply explores the nature of the knowledge required to attain spiritual liberation. The term Adhyatma refers to all that concerns the soul, the Self, the inner dimension of existence. Vidya means knowledge or wisdom. This work focuses on the idea that true knowledge is not that which pertains to the outer world, but that which concerns our deepest nature—our immortal being, which is identical with Brahman, the Absolute.

In Adhyatma Vidya, Shankaracharya guides the reader through the process of liberation from suffering and ignorance (avidya), which arise from false identification with body, mind, and emotions. The work centers on direct knowledge of the Self (Atman) and the recognition of its unity with Brahman, the ultimate, transcendent, and impersonal reality that pervades the entire universe.

Spiritual Knowledge as the Path to Liberation

In Adhyatma Vidya, Shankaracharya distinguishes between two types of knowledge: empirical knowledge, which pertains to the external world and the phenomenal reality, and spiritual knowledge, which concerns the Self and the absolute truth. Spiritual knowledge—Adhyatma Vidya—is seen as the only means to attain moksha (liberation) from the cycle of birth, death, and suffering (samsara). This knowledge is not acquired through the senses or intellect, but through direct experience, contemplation, and inner realization.

According to Shankaracharya, true knowledge is that which allows us to recognize that the Atman, the individual Self, is not separate from Brahman, the ultimate reality. The Self, which is eternal and immutable, is the very substance of the universe. Liberation occurs when the practitioner realizes that the apparent separation between self and world is an illusion—born of ignorance—that veils the true perception of the Self.

The Nature of Atman and the Awakening to Truth

Adhyatma Vidya explores the fundamental concept that the Self (Atman) is identical to Brahman. While body and mind are transient phenomena, the Atman is eternal, unchanging, and formless. Spiritual knowledge implies awakening to the awareness that our true being is divine, and that all forms of separation are mere projections of the illusory mind.

Awakening to the truth of the Self is not merely an intellectual act, but an experience that transcends the mind and intellect. Adhyatma Vidya teaches that the realization of the Self is the direct experience of Brahman, which is the fundamental, all-pervading principle of the universe. When this realization is attained, there is no longer any duality between subject and object, between knower and known. Separation ceases to exist, and unity with all that is becomes a living experience.

Maya and the Illusion of Separation

A central theme of Adhyatma Vidya is the illusory nature of the perceived separation between the individual Self and the universe. Shankaracharya affirms that the phenomenal world we perceive through the senses is a result of Maya, illusion. The separation between the individual and the world, between Atman and Brahman, is merely a projection of the mind, which—through ignorance (avidya)—creates a sense of duality.

According to Shankaracharya, this ignorance is the root cause of suffering and of the cycle of birth and death. The individual identifies with the body and mind, believing themselves to be separate from the rest of the universe. However, Adhyatma Vidya teaches that this separation is an illusion, and that the true reality is the unity of the Self with Brahman.

Awakening to the truth of Adhyatma Vidya means recognizing that there is no separation between the individual and the Divine. The awareness that all is one brings an end to suffering and the beginning of eternal peace, which is the very nature of Brahman.

The Role of Meditation in Spiritual Knowledge

In Adhyatma Vidya, meditation is seen as a fundamental tool for awakening to Self-knowledge. Meditating on the Self involves withdrawing the mind from the distractions of the outer world and focusing on one's inner essence. Meditation helps purify the mind from the illusions of Maya and cultivates the clarity needed to recognize our unity with Brahman.

Meditation is also the means through which ignorance is dissolved. Shankaracharya emphasizes that the mind must be quiet and focused in order to realize the truth, for mental distractions and illusions obscure the perception of ultimate reality. Introspection, awareness, and contemplation of the Self are practices that allow us to realize our divine nature.

Liberation Through Spiritual Knowledge

Liberation (moksha) is the culmination of Adhyatma Vidya. Liberation is not something to be attained in the future, but the awakening to the awareness of our eternal nature. Shankaracharya teaches that liberation is the cessation of suffering caused by ignorance and separation. When it is realized that the Atman is identical to Brahman, the duality between subject and object dissolves, and the individual attains eternal peace.

Awareness of the Self is liberating because it frees us from the chains of illusion and separation. Realization of Brahman—which is all-pervading and undifferentiated—is the truth that sets us free. Shankaracharya teaches that liberation is not an external event or a reward granted to us, but a transformation of our perception of reality that enables us to see the Divine in all things.

Conclusion: Adhyatma Vidya as a Guide to Realization

Shankaracharya's Adhyatma Vidya is a work that guides us directly to the realization of the Self and offers tools to see beyond the illusions of Maya. The ignorance that leads us to perceive ourselves as separate from the Divine is dissolved through spiritual knowledge, which is the direct experience of our divine being. The practice of meditation, the discrimination between what is real and what is illusory, and the awareness of our unity with Brahman are the foundational pillars of Adhyatma Vidya.

Shankaracharya invites us to walk the path to liberation not as an external quest, but as an awakening to the truth already within us. Spiritual knowledge enables us to realize our oneness with the Absolute and to live in peace and harmony with the Divine that permeates every aspect of existence.

CHAPTER 12: MANDUKYA KARIKA

The Mandukya Karika by Gaudapada, the teacher of Adi Shankaracharya, is one of the foundational texts of Vedanta philosophy. It is a commentary on the brief yet powerful Mandukya Upanishad. Though concise, the Mandukya Upanishad offers a profound exposition of the ultimate reality, symbolized in the sacred syllable Om. In his Karika, Gaudapada expands and interprets the doctrines of this Upanishad, and Shankaracharya provides further commentary to make the non-dualistic (Advaita) philosophy more accessible and comprehensible.

The Mandukya Upanishad and the Symbol Om

The Mandukya Upanishad stands apart from other Upanishads due to its brevity and the density of its content. In just twelve verses, it presents the relationship between the sacred sound Om and consciousness, outlining the different states of human experience. According to the Mandukya Upanishad, Om is the symbol that encapsulates all of creation and reflects the absolute truth. This primordial sound is not merely a phonetic marker but a representation of universal consciousness—of Brahman, the ultimate, formless, and undifferentiated reality.

The Mandukya Upanishad divides the sound Om into four states of consciousness: Vaisvanara (waking), Taijasa (dream), Prajna (deep sleep), and Turiya (pure, transcendent consciousness). Each state represents a different aspect of awareness. In Turiya, the practitioner experiences unity with the Divine—the realization that the Self (Atman) and ultimate reality (Brahman) are inseparable.

Shankaracharya's Interpretation of the Mandukya Karika

In the Mandukya Karika, Shankaracharya expands the meaning of these states of consciousness, introducing the idea that the perceived separation between subject (Atman) and object (Brahman) is illusory—a product of Maya, the illusion that creates the appearance of a phenomenal world distinct from ultimate reality. He teaches that the perception of reality as multiplicity is the result of ignorance (Avidya), and that only through direct knowledge and inner experience can this illusion be overcome.

In his commentary, Shankaracharya explains that consciousness is a unified and indivisible phenomenon. Though it appears fragmented into states such as waking, dreaming, and deep sleep, in truth all these are expressions of the same universal consciousness. The distinction between Atman (individual Self) and Brahman (ultimate reality) is only apparent and is dissolved through direct realization of one's essence.

The Four States of Consciousness: A Deeper Insight

1. Vaisvanara (Waking State)

This is the state in which we are aware of the external world through the senses. Here, the perception of the physical world dominates, and we identify with the body and mind. In this state, we are engaged in worldly activity but remain disconnected from the awareness of our deeper essence.

2. Taijasa (Dream State)

The dream state is one where the mind remains active while external perception fades. The subject perceives a world projected by their own mind. Taijasa represents the internal experience manifested as mental imagery. The boundary between subject and object becomes less defined, yet full realization has not yet occurred.

3. Prajna (Deep Sleep State)

In this state, the mind is fully withdrawn. There is no awareness of the external world or internal impressions. It is a state of "non-awareness," but not of unconsciousness. The ego and distinctions between subject and object vanish, but complete realization has not yet taken place.

4. Turiya (Pure Consciousness)

Turiya is the fourth state, beyond waking, dreaming, and deep sleep. It is pure, non-dual consciousness, where there is no distinction between subject and object. It is the state of realization in which one experiences unity with the Divine. Turiya is the awareness of ultimate reality—Brahman—unmediated by mind or senses.

Shankaracharya teaches that Turiya is the ultimate truth, while the other states are transient and illusory. The awareness of Turiya is the realization of the Self (Atman) as one with Brahman, the Absolute. It is the experience of non-duality that leads to liberation (moksha).

Maya: The Illusion of the Phenomenal World

One of the central themes of the Mandukya Karika is Maya, the illusion that veils ultimate reality. Shankaracharya explains that the phenomenal world we perceive through the senses is merely a temporary and illusory manifestation of the universal reality. Our everyday experiences, the division between subject and object, the separation of body and mind—all are caused by Maya. Ignorance (Avidya) is the root of this illusion and prevents us from recognizing our true nature.

He teaches that the perceived separation between Atman and Brahman is a mistake born of limited perception and a conditioned mind. True realization occurs when one recognizes that there is no separation between the individual and the universe—that the Self and ultimate reality are one and the same.

The Sound Om: Symbol of Non-Duality

The sound Om is one of the most fascinating and significant aspects of the Mandukya Karika. Shankaracharya explores how Om not only represents the various states of consciousness but also symbolizes Brahman itself. Om is the primordial sound—the cosmic vibration from which the entire universe originates. Every sound, every word, every form in the manifest world is an expression of Om, which is both the cause and the substance of creation. Meditation on Om is therefore a means to realize non-duality and come to know the Self.

According to Shankaracharya, by meditating on Om, the practitioner transcends the limitations of mind and senses and enters the pure awareness of Brahman. Om represents the unity of all things, and through it, one can awaken to the truth and recognize one's identity with the Absolute.

Self-Realization and Liberation

Shankaracharya's philosophy, as expressed in the Mandukya Karika, guides us toward the realization that Atman—our true Self—is identical to Brahman. Liberation (moksha) is not something to be acquired, but something to be recognized. It is the realization that the individual Self has never been separate from the ultimate reality—that the illusion of separation is born of ignorance.

In the Mandukya Karika, Shankaracharya invites us to transcend the dualistic experience of life and recognize our true nature. Self-realization is the experience of non-duality, the experience of complete unity with the Divine—and this realization brings freedom from suffering and the cycle of death.

Conclusion

The Mandukya Karika of Shankaracharya offers one of the deepest explorations of consciousness and ultimate reality. He guides us in understanding the four states of consciousness and shows how, through meditation on Om, we can realize non-duality and unity with Brahman. His philosophy teaches that the separation between Self and the Divine is an illusion, and that true realization is the awareness that we are already one with Brahman.

CHAPTER 13: THE MINOR WORKS OF ADI SHANKARACHARYA

Adi Shankaracharya not only composed deeply philosophical works but also authored a number of shorter texts known as Prakarana Granthas, which serve as introductory treatises on the fundamental principles of Advaita Vedanta. Though brief, these writings are profoundly significant for those who wish to understand the foundations of Shankaracharya's non-dualistic philosophy in a clear and accessible manner.

1. Prakarana Granthas: An Introduction to Vedanta

The Prakarana Granthas are a series of concise treatises that clearly and directly present the key concepts of Advaita Vedanta. These texts are intended for newcomers to Vedantic philosophy who wish to explore the core ideas of non-duality, liberation, and the nature of Atman and Brahman. Though short in length, the Prakarana Granthas offer essential and profound insights into spiritual truth.

2. Anandalahari: Bliss as an Expression of the Divine

Anandalahari is a work that explores the concept of Ananda (bliss) as a manifestation of Brahman, the ultimate reality. The title itself means "The Wave of Bliss," and the text describes how true joy and fulfillment arise from the awareness of the Self as Atman, which is identical to Brahman. In this work, Shankaracharya invites us to recognize universal bliss—not as fleeting emotional states or sensory pleasures, but as an intrinsic quality of being.

The text develops the view that Ananda is not a temporary experience but an eternal principle that permeates all existence. It represents the highest state of realization, in which the individual, through meditation and awareness, experiences unity with the Divine. Joy, in this context, is not limited or conditional, but a radiant expression of the Absolute that transcends duality.

In Anandalahari, Shankaracharya teaches that bliss is the reflection of the knowledge of one's unity with Brahman, and that only through the realization of this unity can one experience enduring peace and happiness. The text is a celebration of the divine joy that flows from the awareness of one's eternal nature.

3. Tattvabodha: An Accessible Guide to Vedantic Knowledge

One of the most well-known treatises among the Prakarana Granthas is Tattvabodha, which means "Knowledge of the Truth." This is a foundational text for anyone who wants to understand the principles of Advaita Vedanta in a clear and practical way. Tattvabodha is a systematic work that introduces the fundamental notions of Vedantic philosophy, such as Atman (the Self), Brahman (the Ultimate Reality), Maya (illusion), and Avidya (ignorance).

In this treatise, Shankaracharya lays out the process by which an individual can realize their identity with Brahman. His approach is logical and progressive, starting with the distinction between the Self and the non-Self, and culminating in the assertion that

Atman is identical to Brahman—the one, absolute reality. The text offers a simple yet comprehensive explanation of the core concepts of Vedanta, making them accessible to readers without a background in formal philosophy.

Tattvabodha is one of the most cherished texts among Shankaracharya's disciples because it provides the foundation for understanding Vedanta in a practical and intelligible way. Through this treatise, the reader is introduced to non-dualistic thought and learns to look beyond the perceived separation between subject and object, between Self and world. Shankaracharya emphasizes the importance of viveka (discrimination) to discern between what is eternal and what is transient, guiding the reader toward an intuitive and spiritual understanding of truth.

The Significance of These Minor Works

Although these shorter works may not be as complex as Shankaracharya's major philosophical commentaries, they are foundational for the spiritual practitioner. They offer an accessible gateway into the philosophy of Advaita Vedanta and serve as a solid basis for meditation and inner practice. These minor treatises are not only philosophical teachings—they are practical tools for Self-realization, inviting the reader to directly experience truth.

In particular, Anandalahari and Tattvabodha are texts that speak both to the mind and the heart, guiding the seeker to perceive the illusory nature of the phenomenal world and to recognize Brahman as the one, eternal, unchanging principle. The blend of philosophy, meditation, and devotion that permeates these texts reflects Shankaracharya's holistic approach, which integrates intellectual insight with the direct experience of the Absolute.

Conclusion

The minor works of Adi Shankaracharya, such as Tattvabodha

and Anandalahari, are masterpieces of Vedantic philosophy that, though brief, encapsulate the essential principles of non-duality. These treatises are fundamental starting points for anyone who wishes to walk the spiritual path of Advaita Vedanta, and they serve as powerful instruments for awakening.

The teaching that emerges from these works is that true knowledge is not conceptual, but a direct experience of non-duality that leads to the realization of the Self. Through his minor works, Adi Shankaracharya offers a practical guide to liberation (moksha), inviting us to recognize that Atman—our innermost essence—is always and already one with Brahman, the Absolute Reality.

CHAPTER 14: DEVOTION AND THE HYMNS OF ADI SHANKARACHARYA

Within the context of Advaita Vedanta, the realization of the Self is not a purely intellectual process, but an experience that embraces the mind, body, and heart. The non-dual path of knowledge as taught by Adi Shankaracharya is distinguished by its holistic approach, which integrates both philosophy and spiritual practice. One of the most powerful forms of this practice is devotion (bhakti), which, although often seen as separate from the path of knowledge, is in truth a fundamental means to transcend the illusion of duality and realize the unity of Atman and Brahman.

The Role of Hymns in Advaita Vedanta

The hymns of Adi Shankaracharya are not merely devotional

praises; they are profound tools aimed at Self-realization. These works channel both devotion and philosophical insight into a single expression, guiding the practitioner toward a direct experience of non-duality. While many are addressed to deities such as Shiva, Vishnu, or the Divine Mother, their deeper meaning lies in the invocation of ultimate reality—the pursuit of Brahman, the Absolute.

Shankaracharya's hymns—such as Bhaja Govindam, Saundarya Lahari, and Nirvana Shatakam—are considered far more than prayers; they are direct invocations of spiritual truth, capable of awakening within the seeker an awareness of the unity between the Self and the Divine. Their power lies not only in their philosophical declarations of non-duality but also in their ability, through repetition and meditation, to lead the practitioner toward the lived experience of that truth.

Hymns as Instruments of Realization

Although Shankaracharya promotes a non-dual philosophical vision, he does not reject devotional expression. On the contrary, he recognizes its importance as a catalyst for inner transformation. His hymns are not in conflict with the path of knowledge—they strengthen it. Chanting these hymns helps purify the mind and focus awareness on the truth that the Divine and the Self are not separate, but different expressions of the same reality.

For example, Bhaja Govindam, one of Shankaracharya's most famous hymns, is not merely a devotional song to Govinda (a form of Vishnu), but a call to renounce worldly vanity and turn the mind toward the Eternal. Similarly, Saundarya Lahari celebrates the beauty of the Divine Mother as an expression of the ultimate reality and creative power, while Nirvana Shatakam describes the inner process through which one recognizes one's identity with Brahman.

The Hymns of Adi Shankaracharya: An Overview

Throughout this book, we will examine several of Shankaracharya's most celebrated hymns in more detail. For now, the following list provides an overview of the primary devotional works he left to the Vedantic tradition:

1. Bhaja Govindam (Moha Mudgara) – A hymn addressed to Vishnu that urges detachment from the material world and devotion to the Eternal.
2. Saundarya Lahari – A hymn to the Divine Mother, rich in tantric and mystical imagery, which celebrates beauty as a divine expression of Brahman.
3. Nirvana Shatakam (Atma Shatakam) – A deeply philosophical hymn that affirms the Self as Brahman and negates all false identifications.
4. Dakshinamurthy Stotram – A hymn to Shiva in his form as the Supreme Guru, who transmits knowledge through silence.
5. Vivekachudamani – Though primarily a philosophical treatise, it contains devotional tones that call for the discernment between the real and the unreal.
6. Anandalahari – A hymn that explores bliss and joy as expressions of the Divine.
7. Tattvabodha – A work that, while didactic and philosophical, includes spiritual reflections guiding the seeker toward Self-realization.
8. Atma Bodha – A concise treatise on Self-awareness, distinguishing between illusion (Maya) and the absolute truth.

These hymns form the vibrant core of Shankaracharya's spiritual vision. They not only convey his non-dual philosophy but, through poetic power, invite the practitioner to live the experience of non-duality.

Conclusion

The hymns of Adi Shankaracharya are powerful tools for spiritual realization. They are not merely prayers but vehicles of transformation—uniting devotion and knowledge to guide the practitioner toward ultimate truth. Though rooted in the Vedic tradition, these hymns are universal in nature, offering those who chant and meditate upon them the opportunity to transcend duality and realize their own divine essence.

In the next chapter, we will delve deeper into each of these hymns, exploring their profound meanings and the influence they continue to exert on the living tradition of Vedantic spirituality.

CHAPTER 15: INTEGRAL HYMNS AND PRESENTATION

Hymns of Adi Shankaracharya

Adi Shankaracharya, in addition to his philosophical treatises, composed numerous hymns of deep spiritual power. These hymns are not mere poetic compositions—they are condensed expressions of the Advaita Vedanta tradition, merging devotion (bhakti), metaphysics, and inner realization. They serve as luminous gateways to the Supreme Truth, and each has the power to awaken the heart, purify the mind, and lead the practitioner toward liberation (moksha).

Here is a concise overview of some of the most significant hymns attributed to him:

1. Bhaja Govindam – This hymn emphasizes devotion to Govinda (a name of Krishna) and highlights the futility of intellectual pursuits without spiritual realization. Composed of 31 verses, it urges the seeker to turn toward the Divine rather than

remain absorbed in fleeting worldly concerns.

2. Nirvana Shatakam (Atma Shatakam) – Consisting of six powerful verses, this hymn declares the nature of the Supreme Self, denying all identification with body, mind, or emotions. It stands as a profound affirmation of Advaita Vedanta's non-dual vision.

3. Dakshinamurthy Stotram – This hymn praises Dakshinamurthy, a form of Shiva as the silent Guru. It explores the illusory nature of the world and the transformative knowledge that leads to liberation.

4. Shiva Panchakshara Stotram – A devotional hymn celebrating the mantra Namah Shivaya. Each verse glorifies one of the five syllables, depicting the attributes and majesty of Shiva.

5. Annapurna Stotram – Dedicated to the goddess Annapurna, a form of Parvati symbolizing nourishment and abundance. The hymn expresses the universe's dependence on her grace and reveres food as a divine gift.

6. Kalabhairavashtakam – A hymn in praise of Kalabhairava, a fierce form of Shiva associated with time and dissolution. It extols his form, attributes, and power to free devotees from fear and illusion.

7. Saundarya Lahari – Translated as "Wave of Beauty," this collection of 100 verses exalts the splendor and grace of Tripura Sundari. It is both a devotional and tantric text, rich in esoteric symbolism and spiritual practices.

8. Manisha Panchakam – Composed of five verses, this hymn affirms the unity of Atman (the individual Self) and Brahman (the Absolute), declaring that the realization of this truth transcends all social and caste distinctions.

□

1. Bhaja Govindam (Worship Govinda)

by Adi Shankaracharya

Bhaja Govindam is one of Adi Shankaracharya's most beloved

hymns—a song of devotion and wisdom that embodies the core message of Advaita Vedanta in poetic form. Also known as Moha Mudgara ("The Hammer of Delusion"), this hymn dismantles the illusions of worldly life and directs the seeker toward the Supreme Truth.

According to tradition, Shankaracharya composed this hymn after observing an old scholar engrossed in the study of Sanskrit grammar. Recognizing that academic knowledge alone could not lead to salvation, especially at the time of death, he spontaneously recited these verses to awaken the man to the true pursuit of the Absolute.

Bhaja Govindam is not merely an appeal to devotion, but a radical call to spiritual awakening. It teaches that the pursuits of wealth, power, and intellectual pride are ultimately empty if they do not lead to the recognition of one's divine nature. Through its simple yet profound verses, Shankaracharya emphasizes impermanence, renunciation, inner peace, and the need to take refuge in the Divine.

Text in Sanskrit, Transliteration, and Translation:

Bhaja Govindam (Worship Govinda)

by Adi Shankaracharya

Verse 1 – The Essence of the Song
भज गोविन्दं भज गोविन्दं गोविन्दं भज मूढमते ।
सम्प्राप्ते सन्निहिते काले न हि न हि रक्षति डुकृञ्करणे ॥ १॥
Bhaja Govindaṁ bhaja Govindaṁ Govindaṁ bhaja mūḍhamate |
Samprāpte sannihite kāle na hi na hi rakṣati ḍukṛñkaraṇe || 1 ||

Worship Govinda, worship Govinda, O foolish mind!
When death approaches, no grammar rule will save you.

Verse 2 – The Illusion of Wealth
मूढ जहीहि धनागमतृष्णां कुरु सद्बुद्धिं मनसि वितृष्णाम् ।
यल्लभसे निजकर्मोपात्तं वित्तं तेन विनोदय चित्तम् ॥ २॥

Mūḍha jahi hi dhanāgama-tṛṣṇāṁ kuru sadbuddhiṁ manasi vitṛṣṇām |
Yallabhase nija-karma-upāttaṁ vittaṁ tena vinodaya cittam || 2 ||

O fool, renounce the insatiable craving for wealth.
Be content with what you have earned through your destiny.

Verse 3 – The Unreliability of Life
नारीस्तनभर नाभीदेशं दृष्ट्वा मा गा मोहावेशम् ।
एतन्मांसवसादि विकारं मनसि विचिन्तय वारं वारम् ॥ ३॥
Nārī-stana-bhara-nābhī-deśaṁ dṛṣṭvā mā gā moha-āveśam |
Etan māṁsa-vasādi vikāraṁ manasi vicintaya vāram vāram || 3 ||

Do not be deluded by the beauty of the female body.
Understand that it is merely flesh and bone, subject to decay.

Verse 4 – Attachment to Family Life
बालस्तावत् क्रीडासक्तः तरुणस्तावत् तरुणीसक्तः ।
वृद्धस्तावत् चिन्तासक्तः परमे ब्रह्मणि कोऽपि न सक्तः ॥ ४॥
Bālas tāvat krīḍāsaktaḥ taruṇas tāvat taruṇī-saktaḥ |
Vṛddhas tāvat cintāsaktaḥ parame brahmaṇi ko'pi na saktaḥ || 4 ||

As a child, one is attached to play; as a youth, to women;
As an old man, to worries—yet no one is devoted to Brahman!

Verse 5 – The Uncertainty of Life
काते कान्ता कस्ते पुत्रः संसारोऽयमतीव विचित्रः ।
कस्य त्वं कः कुत आयातः तत्सं चिन्तय यदिह भ्रातः ॥ ५॥
Kā te kāntā kas te putraḥ saṁsāro'yam atīva vicitraḥ |
Kasya tvaṁ kaḥ kuta āyātaḥ tat samcintaya yadiha bhrātaḥ || 5 ||

Who is your wife? Who is your son?
This world is a strange illusion—reflect on who you truly are.

Verse 6 – The Call to Discernment
सत्सङ्गत्वे निःसङ्गत्वं निःसङ्गत्वे निर्मोहत्वम् ।
निर्मोहत्वे निश्चलतत्त्वं निश्चलतत्त्वे जीवनमुक्तिः ॥ ६॥
Satsaṅgatve nissaṅgatvaṁ nissaṅgatve nirmohatvam |
Nirmohatve niścalatattvaṁ niścalatattve jīvanmuktiḥ || 6 ||

From the company of the wise comes detachment;
From detachment, freedom from delusion;
From freedom from delusion, the unshakable truth—
And through that, liberation while living.

Verse 7 – The True Treasure
गेयम् गीता नाम सहस्रं ध्येयं श्रीपति रूपमजस्रम् ।
नेयं सज्जन सङ्गे चित्तं देयं दीनजनाय च वित्तम् ॥ ७॥
Geyam Gītā-nāma-sahasraṁ dhyeyaṁ Śrīpati-rūpam ajasram |
Neyaṁ sajjana-saṅge cittam deyaṁ dīnajanāya ca vittam || 7 ||

Chant the Gita and the thousand holy names of the Lord,
Meditate constantly on the form of Govinda,
Offer your mind to the company of the noble,
And your wealth to those in need.

Verse 8 – Final Call to Devotion
गुरुचरणाम्बुजनिर्भरभक्तः संसारादचिराद्भव मुक्तः ।
सेन्द्रियमानस नियमादेवं दृष्ट्वा यद्यथार्थमुक्तः ॥ ८॥
Guru-caraṇāmbuja-nirbhara-bhaktaḥ saṁsārād acirād bhava muktaḥ |
Sendriya-mānasa-niyamād evaṁ dṛṣṭvā yady athārtham uktaḥ || 8 ||

One who has unwavering devotion to the lotus feet of the Guru
Soon becomes free from the cycle of birth and death.
By mastering the senses and the mind,
He realizes the Supreme Truth as it truly is.

Conclusion

Bhaja Govindam is a hymn that shatters the illusion of worldly life and calls us to seek the Ultimate Truth. Through simple and direct words, Adi Shankaracharya urges us to renounce attachment to material possessions, transient relationships, and ego, and instead focus on the true essence of existence: Self-realization.

With these immortal verses, Shankaracharya weaves Vedantic

wisdom and devotion into a powerful call to awakening, freedom, and spiritual illumination.

2. Nirvana Shatakam (The Six Verses of Liberation)

by Adi Shankaracharya

Nirvana Shatakam is one of Adi Shankaracharya's most profound and celebrated hymns, composed of six verses that express the direct realization of Advaita Vedanta. This hymn negates all identification with the body, mind, emotions, and the phenomenal world, culminating in the affirmation of one's true nature as Shiva—pure, absolute consciousness.

According to tradition, Adi Shankaracharya composed this hymn when, still a young boy, he met his teacher Govindapada, who asked him, "Who are you?" (Ko bhavan?). In response, the young Shankara sang these verses, revealing his enlightenment.

□

Text in Sanskrit, Transliteration, and Translation

□

Verse 1 – I am neither the body nor the mind
मनो बुद्ध्यहङ्कार चित्तानि नाहं
न च श्रोत्र जिह्वे न च घ्राण नेत्रे ।
न च व्योम भूमिर्न तेजो न वायुः
चिदानन्द रुपः शिवोऽहम् शिवोऽहम् ॥ १॥

Mano buddhyahaṅkāra cittāni nāhaṁ
Na ca śrotra jihve na ca ghrāṇa netre |
Na ca vyoma bhūmir na tejo na vāyuḥ
Cidānanda rūpaḥ śivo'ham śivo'ham || 1 ||

I am not the mind, the intellect, the ego, or the memory.
I am not the sense of hearing, taste, smell, or sight.
I am not the elements—ether, earth, fire, or air.
I am the form of pure consciousness and bliss. I am Shiva, I am

Shiva.

▯

Verse 2 – I am not emotions nor the senses
न च प्राण संज्ञो न वै पञ्चवायु:
न वा सप्तधातुः न वा पञ्चकोशः ।
न वाक्पाणि पादं न चोपस्थपायु:
चिदानन्द रूपः शिवोऽहम् शिवोऽहम् ॥ २॥

Na ca prāṇa saṁjño na vai pañca-vāyuḥ
Na vā sapta-dhātuḥ na vā pañca-kośaḥ |
Na vāk pāṇi pādaṁ na copastha-pāyuḥ
Cidānanda rūpaḥ śivo'ham śivo'ham || 2 ||

I am not breath, nor the five vital airs.
I am not the seven bodily elements, nor the five sheaths.
I am not speech, hands, feet, nor the organs of procreation or elimination.
I am the form of pure consciousness and bliss. I am Shiva, I am Shiva.

▯

Verse 3 – I am beyond desire and attachment
न मे द्वेष रागौ न मे लोभ मोहौ
मदो नैव मे नैव मात्सर्य भावः ।
न धर्मो न चार्थो न कामो न मोक्षः
चिदानन्द रूपः शिवोऽहम् शिवो'हम् ॥ ३॥

Na me dveṣa rāgau na me lobha mohau
Mado naiva me naiva mātsarya bhāvaḥ |
Na dharmo na cārtho na kāmo na mokṣaḥ
Cidānanda rūpaḥ śivo'ham śivo'ham || 3 ||

I have neither hatred nor attachment, nor greed nor delusion.
I have no pride, no jealousy, no desire for superiority.
I am not Dharma, Artha, Kama, or Moksha.
I am the form of pure consciousness and bliss. I am Shiva, I am

Shiva.

□

Verse 4 – I have no birth nor death
न जन्म न मृत्यु न संघर्षो मे
न माता न पिता न च जन्मः न बन्धुः ।
न मित्रं न शत्रु न शिष्यं न गुरुः
चिदानन्द रूपः शिवोऽहम् शिवो'हम् ॥ ४॥

Na janma na mṛtyu na saṁgharṣo me
Na mātā na pitā na ca janmaḥ na bandhuḥ |
Na mitraṁ na śatru na śiṣyaṁ na guruḥ
Cidānanda rūpaḥ śivo'ham śivo'ham || 4 ||

I have no birth, no death, and no inner struggle.
I have no mother, no father, and no origin.
I have no relatives, friends, enemies, disciples, or teacher.
I am the form of pure consciousness and bliss. I am Shiva, I am Shiva.

□

Verse 5 – I transcend time and space
अहं निर्विकल्पो निराकार रूपः
विभुर्व्याप्य सर्वत्र सर्वेन्द्रियाणाम् ।
सदा मे समत्वं न मुक्तिः न बन्धः
चिदानन्द रूपः शिवोऽहम् शिवो'हम् ॥ ५॥

Ahaṁ nirvikalpo nirākāra rūpaḥ
Vibhur vyāpya sarvatra sarvendriyāṇām |
Sadā me samatvaṁ na muktiḥ na bandhaḥ
Cidānanda rūpaḥ śivo'ham śivo'ham || 5 ||

I am changeless, formless, and without limitation.
I am all-pervasive, beyond all the senses.
I remain always in equanimity, knowing neither liberation nor bondage.
I am the form of pure consciousness and bliss. I am Shiva, I am

Shiva.

□

Verse 6 – I am eternal, pure consciousness
न भोगं न योगं न वेदं न यज्ञं
न मंत्रं न तीर्थं न वेदाः न यज्ञाः ।
अहं भोज्यं न भोक्तृ न भोक्तं न भोगः
चिदानन्द रूपः शिवोऽहम् शिवो'हम् ॥ ६॥

Na bhogaṁ na yogaṁ na vedaṁ na yajñaṁ
Na mantraṁ na tīrthaṁ na vedāḥ na yajñāḥ |
Ahaṁ bhojyaṁ na bhoktṛ na bhoktaṁ na bhogaḥ
Cidānanda rūpaḥ śivo'ham śivo'ham || 6 ||

I am not sensory pleasure, nor the practice of Yoga.
I am not the Vedas nor the sacrificial rites.
I am not the food, the one who eats, nor the act of eating.
I am the form of pure consciousness and bliss. I am Shiva, I am Shiva.

□

Conclusion

Nirvana Shatakam is one of the most powerful and direct declarations of Advaitic realization. In these verses, Shankaracharya negates all identification with body, mind, emotions, relationships, time, and space, affirming the true nature of being as pure consciousness beyond all duality.

The final phrase—I am Shiva, I am Shiva (Shivo'ham Shivo'ham)—does not refer to the deity Shiva, but to absolute awareness, to the Atman, which is identical with Brahman.

This hymn is a radical affirmation of spiritual freedom, dissolving all illusion and inviting us to recognize our true nature as pure existence, consciousness, and bliss (Sat-Chit-Ananda).

3. Dakshinamurthy Stotram

(Hymn to Dakshinamurthy, the Silent Guru)
by Adi Shankaracharya

This hymn by Adi Shankaracharya is one of the highest expressions of Advaita Vedanta philosophy, in which Dakshinamurthy, the silent form of Shiva as the Supreme Guru, transmits the knowledge of the Absolute through silence.

Text in Sanskrit, Transliteration, and Translation

Verse 1
सर्वविद्यानामाधारं भुवनगुरुमीशं शिवं दक्षिणामूर्तिम्।
नमाम्यहं सदानन्दं गुरुमज्ञानद्वान्तदीपं तम्॥

sarva-vidyānām ādhāraṃ bhuvana-gurum īśaṃ śivaṃ dakṣiṇāmūrtim |
namāmy ahaṃ sadānandaṃ gurum ajñāna-dvānta-dīpaṃ tam ||

I bow to Dakshinamurthy, the silent Guru,
The foundation of all knowledge, the teacher of the world,
The embodiment of Shiva, the eternal light of wisdom,
Who dispels the darkness of ignorance.

Verse 2
विषयं परिहास्यन्तं जगदपि स्वप्नवत्पश्यन्तं
ज्ञानं हि परमार्थसत्यमिति यो वक्ति सः दक्षिणामूर्तिः॥

viṣayaṃ parihāsyantaṃ jagad api svapnavat paśyantaṃ |
jñānaṃ hi paramārtha-satyam iti yo vakti saḥ dakṣiṇāmūrtiḥ ||

He who sees the world as a fleeting dream,
And declares that only supreme knowledge is real—
He is Dakshinamurthy, the silent Guru,
Who reveals illusion and points to the Absolute.

Verse 3
मायावीव विजृम्भयत्यपि महायोगीव यः स्वेच्छया
तस्मै श्रीगुरवे नमोऽस्तु सततं श्रीदक्षिणामूर्तये॥

māyāvīva vijṛmbhayaty api mahā-yogīva yaḥ svecchayā |
tasmai śrī-gurave namo'stu satataṃ śrī-dakṣiṇāmūrtaye ||

The universe unfolds like the play of Maya,
Like a great Yogi expressing himself by his own will.
To him, the Supreme Guru, I bow forever—
To Dakshinamurthy, the silent master of Oneness.

Verse 4
शरीरं स्वप्नसदृशं यत्पश्यति योगिनाम्।
ज्ञानं च तदसत्सर्वं स एव दक्षिणामूर्तिः॥

śarīraṃ svapna-sadṛśaṃ yat paśyati yogināṃ |
jñānaṃ ca tad asat sarvaṃ sa eva dakṣiṇāmūrtiḥ ||

The enlightened yogi sees the body as dreamlike,
And all empirical knowledge as unreal.
He who realizes this truth is Dakshinamurthy—
The eternal Self beyond all appearances.

Verse 5
गुरुं योगेश्वरं शान्तं ज्ञानस्वरूपमद्वयम्।
नमाम्यहमहं वन्दे दक्षिणामूर्तिमीदृशम्॥

guruṃ yogeśvaraṃ śāntaṃ jñāna-svarūpam advayam |
namāmy aham ahaṃ vande dakṣiṇāmūrtim īdṛśam ||

To the Guru, Lord of Yoga, infinite peace,
Essence of non-dual knowledge—
With complete devotion, I bow
To Dakshinamurthy, eternal presence of the Self.

Verse 6
आसन्नो दूरिकं तत्त्वं तत्त्वं तस्मिन्यथासति।
श्रीदक्षिणामूर्तिर्यः स एव परमेश्वरः॥

āsanno dūrikaṃ tattvaṃ tattvaṃ tasmin yathāsati |
śrī-dakṣiṇāmūrtir yaḥ sa eva parameśvaraḥ ||

To one who seeks outside, the Absolute appears distant;

To one who turns within, it is nearer than breath.
Dakshinamurthy is this living truth—
He is the Supreme Lord beyond all separation.

Verse 7
चिन्मात्रं भासयत्येवं नामरूपविवर्जितम्।
यस्मै स गुरवे नित्यं नमः श्रीदक्षिणामूर्तये॥

cin-mātraṃ bhāsayaty evaṃ nāma-rūpa-vivarjitam |
yasmai sa gurave nityaṃ namaḥ śrī-dakṣiṇāmūrtaye ||

The essence of consciousness shines beyond name and form,
Light without beginning or end, beyond thought and time.
To that eternal Guru I bow—
To Dakshinamurthy, the pure consciousness that illuminates all.

Verse 8
नाहं देहो न च प्राणो न च मनोग्राह्यभावः।
शुद्धं ज्ञानस्वरूपं तत्साक्षाद्दक्षिणामूर्तिः॥

nāhaṃ deho na ca prāṇo na ca mano-grāhya-bhāvaḥ |
śuddhaṃ jñāna-svarūpaṃ tat sākṣād dakṣiṇāmūrtiḥ ||

I am not the body, nor breath, nor the mind's grasped objects.
I am pure awareness that pervades all things.
This is the direct realization of Dakshinamurthy—
The eternal consciousness reflected in every being.

Verse 9
नित्योऽहं परमानन्दो ज्ञानानन्दमयोऽहम्।
श्रीदक्षिणामूर्तिर्योऽहमहं गुरुरेव च॥

nityo'haṃ paramānando jñānānanda-mayo'ham |
śrī-dakṣiṇāmūrtir yo'ham ahaṃ gurur eva ca ||

I am eternal, supreme bliss,
Pure knowledge and infinite joy.
I am Dakshinamurthy himself—
The very essence of the Guru, formless and free.

Deeper Meaning of the Hymn

- Dakshinamurthy is the Supreme Guru, who transmits the knowledge of the Absolute through silence.
- The hymn portrays the world as a dream, and the ultimate truth as eternal consciousness beyond body and mind.
- The Guru is not separate from the disciple: the true Master is the Self.
- The Self is beyond time, duality, name, and form.
- The final realization is: "I am Shiva", "I am Brahman".

4. Śiva Pañcākṣara Stotram

(Hymn of the Five Sacred Syllables to Śiva, by Adi Shankaracharya)

This hymn is dedicated to the mantra "Namaḥ Śivāya" (नमः शिवाय), composed of five sacred syllables: Na, Ma, Śi, Vā, Ya. Each verse of the text praises one of these syllables and its profound significance.

□

Text in Sanskrit, Transliteration, and Translation

□

Verse 1 – NA
नागेन्द्रहाराय त्रिलोचनाय
भस्माङ्गरागाय महेश्वराय ।
नित्याय शुद्धाय दिगम्बराय
तस्मै नकाराय नमः शिवाय ॥ १॥

Nāgendra-hārāya trilocanāya
Bhasmāṅga-rāgāya maheśvarāya |
Nityāya śuddhāya digambarāya
Tasmai nakārāya namaḥ śivāya || 1 ||

Salutations to Śiva, adorned with the mighty serpent as his garland,

The three-eyed One whose body is anointed with sacred ash.
He is eternal, pure, and robed in the directions alone.
To Him, symbolized by the syllable Na, I bow in devotion.

Verse 2 – MA
मन्दाकिनीसलिलचन्दनचर्चिताय
नन्दीश्वरप्रमथनाथमहेश्वराय ।
मन्दारपुष्पबहुपूजिताय
तस्मै मकाराय नमः शिवाय ॥ २॥

Mandākinī-salila-candana-carcitāya
Nandīśvara-pramatha-nātha-maheśvarāya |
Mandāra-puṣpa-bahu-pūjitāya
Tasmai makārāya namaḥ śivāya || 2 ||

Salutations to Śiva, anointed with the sacred waters of the Ganges and cooling sandal paste,
Lord of Nandi and the celestial hosts, the supreme Maheshvara.
Adored with countless mandara flowers,
To Him, symbolized by the syllable Ma, I bow in devotion.

Verse 3 – ŚI
शिवाय गौरीवदनाब्जवृन्द
सूर्याय दक्षिणामूर्तये नमः ।
नमः शान्ताय घनशामलाय
तस्मै शिकाराय नमः शिवाय ॥ ३॥

Śivāya gaurī-vadanābja-vṛnda
Sūryāya dakṣiṇāmūrtaye namaḥ |
Namaḥ śāntāya ghana-śyāmalāya
Tasmai śikārāya namaḥ śivāya || 3 ||

Salutations to Śiva, beloved of Gaurī, whose face is as radiant as a blooming lotus,
Radiant as the sun, the supreme Guru Dakshinamurthy.

He is the embodiment of peace, with a deep blue hue like rain clouds.
To Him, symbolized by the syllable Śi, I bow in devotion.

□

Verse 4 – VĀ
वसिष्ठकुम्भोद्भवगौतमार्य
मुनीन्द्रदेवार्चितशेखराय ।
चन्द्रार्कवैश्वानरलोचनाय
तस्मै वकाराय नमः शिवाय ॥ ४॥

Vasiṣṭha-kumbhodbhava-gautamārya
Munīndra-devārcita-śekharāya |
Candrārka-vaiśvānara-locanāya
Tasmai vakārāya namaḥ śivāya || 4 ||

Salutations to Śiva, honored by sages like Vasiṣṭha, Agastya, and Gautama,
Worshiped by the seers and gods as the Supreme Lord.
He whose eyes are the moon, the sun, and the sacred fire—
To Him, symbolized by the syllable Vā, I bow in devotion.

□

Verse 5 – YA
यज्ञस्वरूपाय जटाधराय
पिनाकहस्ताय सनातनाय ।
दिव्याय देवाय दिगम्बराय
तस्मै यकाराय नमः शिवाय ॥ ५॥

Yajña-svarūpāya jaṭā-dharāya
Pināka-hastāya sanātanāya |
Divyāya devāya digambarāya
Tasmai yakārāya namaḥ śivāya || 5 ||

Salutations to Śiva, the very embodiment of sacrifice,
He who wears matted locks and wields the trident Pināka.
Eternal, divine, and unbounded by any form—

To Him, symbolized by the syllable Ya, I bow in devotion.

▯

Deeper Meaning of the Mantra and the Hymn

The mantra Namaḥ Śivāya is one of the most sacred in Hinduism and expresses the essence of divine consciousness. The Śiva Pañcākṣara Stotram glorifies this sacredness, unveiling the mystical meaning behind the five syllables:

1. Na (न) – Symbolizes detachment from worldly bonds and reverence for Śiva.
2. Ma (म) – Represents the purification of the soul through service and devotion.
3. Śi (शि) – Signifies union with the Absolute and true knowledge.
4. Vā (वा) – Indicates cosmic awareness and spiritual illumination.
5. Ya (य) – Represents the individual soul merging with the divine.

Each syllable holds the power of mokṣa (liberation) and self-realization.

▯

Conclusion

- Adi Shankaracharya composed this hymn to help devotees contemplate and meditate upon the mantra Namaḥ Śivāya.
- It represents inner transformation and the awakening of supreme consciousness.
- Reciting or meditating on this hymn brings peace, strength, and illumination.

5. Annapūrṇa Stotram

(Hymn to the Goddess Annapūrṇa, by Adi Shankaracharya)

The Annapūrṇa Stotram is a hymn dedicated to Goddess Annapūrṇa, the form of Pārvatī who symbolizes nourishment and abundance. Her name means "She who fills with food" and represents the divine principle that sustains life through both physical and spiritual nourishment.

▯

Text in Sanskrit, Transliteration, and Translation

▯

Verse 1
नित्याऽनन्दकरी वराभयकरी सौन्दर्यरत्नाकरी
निर्धूताखिलघोरपावनकरी प्रत्यक्षमाहेश्वरी।
प्रालेयाचलवंशपावनकरी काशीपुराधीश्वरी
भिक्षां देहि कृपावलम्बनकरी माताऽन्नपूर्णेश्वरी ॥ १॥

Nityānandakari varābhayakari saundarya-ratnākari
Nirdhūtākhila-ghora-pāvanakari pratyakṣa-māheśvarī |
Prāleyācala-vaṁśa-pāvanakari kāśīpurādhīśvarī
Bhikṣāṁ dehi kṛpāvalambanakari māt'ānnapūrṇeśvarī || 1 ||

O Goddess Annapūrṇa, granter of eternal bliss,
She who bestows boons and protection,
A treasure of divine beauty and grace,
She who purifies from all terrible evils and leads to liberation.
Sovereign of the sacred city of Kāśī,
Grant me your grace and blessing,
O Mother Annapūrṇa, ocean of compassion!

▯

Verse 2
नानारत्नविचित्रभूषणकरी हेमाम्बराडम्बरि
मुक्ताहारविलम्बमानविलसद्वक्षोजकुम्भान्तरी।
काश्मीरागरुवासिता रुचिकरी काशीपुराधीश्वरी
भिक्षां देहि कृपावलम्बनकरी माताऽन्नपूर्णेश्वरी ॥ २॥

Nānāratna-vicitra-bhūṣaṇakari hemāmbarāḍambarī
Muktāhāra-vilambamāna-vilasad-vakṣoja-kumbhāntarī |
Kāśmīrāgaru-vāsitā-rucikari kāśīpurādhīśvarī
Bhikṣāṁ dehi kṛpāvalambanakari māt'ānnapūrṇeśvarī || 2 ||

O Goddess, adorned with radiant jewels and draped in golden garments,
Whose divine form glows with the brilliance of pearl necklaces,
Scented with the essence of sandalwood and Kashmir musk,
Sovereign of the sacred city of Kāśī,
Grant me your grace and support,
O Mother Annapūrṇa, ocean of compassion!

□

Verse 3
योगानन्दकरी रिपुक्षयकरी धर्मार्थनिष्ठाकरी
चन्द्रार्कानलभासमानलहरी त्रैलोक्यसंहारिणी।
काशीश्वरप्राणनायककरी काशीपुराधीश्वरी
भिक्षां देहि कृपावलम्बनकरी माताऽन्नपूर्णेश्वरी ॥ ३॥

Yogānandakari ripukṣayakari dharmārthanisṭhākari
Candrārkānala-bhāsamāna-laharī trailokya-saṁhāriṇī |
Kāśīśvara-prāṇa-nāyakakari kāśīpurādhīśvarī
Bhikṣāṁ dehi kṛpāvalambanakari māt'ānnapūrṇeśvarī || 3 ||

O Mother Annapūrṇa, who brings joy to yogis,
She who destroys inner enemies and upholds the path of righteousness,
Radiant like the waves of moonlight, sunlight, and fire,
She who dissolves illusions across the three worlds,
Sovereign of the sacred city of Kāśī,
Grant me your grace and your support,
O Mother Annapūrṇa, ocean of compassion!

□

Verse 4

कैलासाचलकन्दमोदनकरी गौरीगणेशेश्वरी
भक्ताभीष्टमुखप्रदायकरी काशीपुराधीश्वरी।
काशीकाश्मरमाणिक्यरुचिकरी काशीपुराधीश्वरी
भिक्षां देहि कृपावलम्बनकरी माताऽन्नपूर्णेश्वरी ॥ ४॥

Kailāsācala-kandamodanakari gaurīgaṇeśeśvarī
Bhaktābhīṣṭa-mukha-pradāyakari kāśīpurādhīśvarī |
Kāśīkāśmara-māṇikya-rucikari kāśīpurādhīśvarī
Bhikṣāṁ dehi kṛpāvalambanakari māt'ānnapūrṇeśvarī || 4 ||

O Annapūrṇa, dwelling on the sacred mountain Kailāśa,
Divine Mother of Gaurī and sovereign of Gaṇeśa,
Fulfiller of the sincere desires of her devotees,
Radiant like sparkling rubies from Kāśī and Kāśmīr,
Sovereign of the sacred city of Kāśī,
Grant me your grace and support,
O Mother Annapūrṇa, ocean of compassion!

▯

Meaning of the Annapūrṇa Stotram

- Annapūrṇa is the aspect of the Divine Mother who provides nourishment and abundance.
- This hymn speaks not only of material food, but of spiritual nourishment—knowledge and Self-realization.
- To ask for her grace means to seek support on the spiritual path and liberation from the cycle of birth and death (saṁsāra).
- "Bhikṣāṁ dehi" means "Grant me alms"—a prayer for her grace and illumination.

▯

Conclusion

The Annapūrṇa Stotram by Adi Shankaracharya is a profound hymn that bridges materiality and spirituality. Asking the Goddess for food is not just a devotional gesture—it symbolizes the quest for knowledge, wisdom, and inner realization.

This hymn is often recited before meals or as a prayer for prosperity and spiritual awakening.

6. Kālabhairavāṣṭakam

(Hymn to Kālabhairava, by Adi Shankaracharya)

The Kālabhairavāṣṭakam is a powerful hymn dedicated to Kālabhairava, one of the fiercest and most transcendent forms of Śiva. Kālabhairava is the Lord of Time (Kāla) and the one who dissolves fear, illusion, and ignorance. He is revered as the protector of Kāśī (Varanasi) and the guardian of ultimate truth.

▯

Text in Sanskrit, Transliteration, and Translation

▯

Verse 1
देवराजसेव्यमानपावनाङ्घ्रिपङ्कजं
व्यालयज्ञसूत्रमिन्दुशेखरं कृपाकरम् ।
नारदादियोगिवृन्दवन्दितं दिगम्बरं
काशिकापुराधिनाथकालभैरवं भजे ॥ १॥

Devarāja-sevyamāna-pāvanāṅghri-paṅkajaṁ
Vyāla-yajña-sūtra-mindu-śekharaṁ kṛpākaram |
Nāradaādi-yogi-vṛnda-vanditaṁ digambaraṁ
Kāśikāpurādhinātha-kālabhairavaṁ bhaje || 1 ||

I worship Kālabhairava, the Lord of Kāśī,
Whose lotus feet are revered by the kings of the gods,
Who wears a serpent as his sacred thread and the moon upon his crown,
The embodiment of compassion, worshipped by Nārada and yogis,
Who wears nothing but the sky as his garment.

□

Verse 2
भानुकोटिभास्वरं भवाब्धितारकं परं
नीलकण्ठमीप्सितार्थदायकं त्रिलोचनम् ।
कालकालमम्बुजाक्षमक्षशूलमक्षरं
काशिकापुराधिनाथकालभैरवं भजे ॥ २॥

Bhānu-koṭi-bhāsvaraṁ bhavābdhi-tārakaṁ paraṁ
Nīlakaṇṭham-īpsitārtha-dāyakaṁ trilocanam |
Kāla-kālam-ambujākṣam-akṣaśūlam-akṣaraṁ
Kāśikāpurādhinātha-kālabhairavaṁ bhaje || 2 ||

I worship Kālabhairava, the Lord of Kāśī,
Radiant like millions of suns, who rescues from the ocean of saṁsāra,
Blue-throated, granter of heartfelt wishes, three-eyed,
Destroyer of Time itself, lotus-eyed, wielder of trident and eternal essence.

□

Verse 3
शूलटङ्कपाशदण्डपाणिमादिकारणं
सर्वपापहरं देवं स्मिताविलासवक्त्रकम् ।
निलदंतिरेगशुद्धिमुद्दतं सनातनं
काशिकापुराधिनाथकालभैरवं भजे ॥ ३॥

Śūlaṭaṅka-pāśa-daṇḍa-pāṇim-ādikāraṇaṁ
Sarvapāpa-haraṁ devaṁ smitāvilāsa-vaktrakam |
Nīlakaṇṭha-rig-śuddhim-uddhataṁ sanātanaṁ
Kāśikāpurādhinātha-kālabhairavaṁ bhaje || 3 ||

I worship Kālabhairava, the Lord of Kāśī,
Who holds the trident, hook, noose, and club—origin of all things,
Remover of all sins, divine with a smiling radiant face,
Blue-throated, pure, and ever eternal.

□

Verse 4
रत्नपादुकाप्रभाभिरामपादयुग्मकं
नित्यसन्मदादिविभ्रमं भुवेज्ञानसायकम् ।
श्रीमत्पद्मवस्त्रितोपभासुरं दयाकरं
काशिकापुराधिनाथकालभैरवं भजे ॥ ४॥

Ratna-pādukā-prabhābhirāma-pāda-yugmakaṁ
Nitya-sanmadādi-vibhramaṁ bhuve jñāna-sāyakam |
Śrīmat-padma-vastritopa-bhāsuraṁ dayākaraṁ
Kāśikāpurādhinātha-kālabhairavaṁ bhaje || 4 ||

I worship Kālabhairava, the Lord of Kāśī,
Whose jeweled sandals shine with celestial brilliance,
He who shatters worldly delusions and bestows divine wisdom,
Radiant in lotus-like attire, source of boundless compassion.

Verse 5
भुक्तिमुक्तिदायकं प्रशस्तचारुविग्रहम्
भक्तवत्सलं स्थितं समस्तलोकविग्रहम् ।
निकन्दकं धनञ्जयादिभूतिविग्रहम्
काशिकापुराधिनाथकालभैरवं भजे ॥ ५॥

Bhukti-mukti-dāyakaṁ praśasta-cāru-vigrahaṁ
Bhakta-vatsalaṁ sthitaṁ samasta-loka-vigrahaṁ |
Nikandakaṁ dhanañjayādi-bhūti-vigrahaṁ
Kāśikāpurādhinātha-kālabhairavaṁ bhaje || 5 ||

I worship Kālabhairava, the Lord of Kāśī,
Granter of both worldly enjoyment and liberation,
Of exquisite form, ever loving to his devotees,
The universal presence, destroyer of enemies and embodiment of victory.

Verse 6
कालभैरवाष्टकं पठन्ति ये मनोहरं

ज्ञानमुक्तिसाधनं विचक्षणां सदा नराः ।
ते लभन्ते कालभैरवस्य पदसेवनं
काशिकापुराधिनाथकालभैरवं भजे ॥ ६॥

Kālabhairavāṣṭakaṁ paṭhanti ye manoharaṁ
Jñāna-mukti-sādhanaṁ vicakṣaṇāṁ sadā narāḥ |
Te labhante kālabhairavasya pada-sevanaṁ
Kāśikāpurādhinātha-kālabhairavaṁ bhaje || 6 ||

Those wise ones who recite this enchanting Kālabhairavāṣṭakam
As a path to knowledge and liberation,
Shall attain the blessed service at the feet of Kālabhairava,
The Lord of Kāśī, the transcendent guardian of truth.

▯

Meaning of the Kālabhairavāṣṭakam

- Kālabhairava is the embodiment of time, dissolution, and transcendence—the aspect of Śiva that destroys ignorance and leads to Self-realization.
- This hymn dispels the fear of death and helps one transcend the cycle of rebirths.
- Reciting this stotram grants protection, wisdom, and liberation (mokṣa).

▯

Conclusion

The Kālabhairavāṣṭakam is one of Adi Shankaracharya's most powerful hymns, invoking the fierce grace of Kālabhairava as the Lord of Time and Transformation. Chanting this hymn brings spiritual protection, inner strength, and ultimate freedom.

7. Saundarya Lahari (The Wave of Beauty)

It consists of one hundred verses:
• The first 41 verses are known as Ananda Lahari (The Waves of Bliss), addressing deep metaphysical and tantric principles.

• The remaining 59 verses (from 42 to 100) form the actual Saundarya Lahari, praising the beauty, grace, and power of the goddess Tripura Sundarī, the supreme aspect of Śakti.

This is a tantric, poetic, and devotional hymn, and each verse is also considered a mantra with transformative power. You have rightly chosen to include it as the pinnacle among the hymns: it is the longest and one of the most powerful.

▯

Sanskrit:
शिवः शक्त्या युक्तो यदि भवति शक्तः प्रभवितुं
न चेदेवं देवो न खलु कुशलः स्पन्दितुमपि।
अतस्त्वां आराध्यां हरिहरविरिञ्चादिभिरपि
प्रणन्तुं स्तोतुं वा कथमकृतपुण्यः प्रभवति॥१॥

Transliteration:
śivaḥ śaktyā yukto yadi bhavati śaktaḥ prabhavituṁ
na ced evaṁ devo na khalu kuśalaḥ spanditum api |
atas tvām ārādhyāṁ harihara-viriñcādibhir api
praṇantuṁ stotuṁ vā katham akṛta-puṇyaḥ prabhavati || 1 ||

Translation:
Only when united with Shakti can Śiva act.
Without Her, even the god is unable to move.
Thus, even Hari, Hara, and Brahmā adore You.
How then can one without accumulated merit ever praise You?

▯

Sanskrit:
तनीयांसं पांसुं तव चरणपङ्केरुहमुहो
शिरस्याघ्रात्ये यं सकलजनिनामुत्तमशिखाम्।
रुचिं तस्याऽऽद्यां कथमिव स हेयस्पदकते
कटाक्षव्याक्षेपं कृतमपि न नैव क्षमयते॥२॥

Transliteration:
tanīyāṁsaṁ pāṁsuṁ tava caraṇa-paṅkeruha-muho

śirasyāghrātya yaṁ sakala-janinām uttama-śikhām |
ruciṁ tasyādyāṁ katham iva sa heya-spada-kate
kaṭākṣa-vyākṣepaṁ kṛtam api na naiva kṣamayate || 2 ||

Translation:
Even one who bows and smells the tiniest dust of Your lotus feet
becomes the crown among all women of creation.
Should such a person reject others,
You do not tolerate even the slightest glance of disdain from them.

▯

Sanskrit:
हरिस्त्वामाराध्य प्रणतजनसौभाग्यजननीं
पुरा नारी भूत्वा पुररिपुमपि क्षोभमनयत्।
स्मरोऽपि त्वां नत्वा रतिनयनलेह्येन वपुषा
मुनीनामप्यन्तः प्रभवति हि मोहाय महताम्॥३॥

Transliteration:
haris tvām ārādhya praṇata-jana-saubhāgya-jananīṁ
purā nārī bhūtvā puraripum api kṣobham anayat |
smaro'pi tvāṁ natvā rati-nayana-lehyena vapuṣā
munīnām apy antaḥ prabhavati hi mohāya mahatām || 3 ||

Translation:
By worshipping You, Viṣṇu once became a woman
and managed to disturb even Śiva, destroyer of the cities.
Even Kāmadeva, bowing before You in a body desired by Rati,
can bewilder the minds of even the highest sages.

▯

Sanskrit:
त्वदीयं सौन्दर्यं तुहिनगिरिकन्ये तुलयितुं
कवीन्द्राः कल्पन्ते कथमपि विरिञ्चिप्रभृतयः।
यदालोकौत्सुक्यादमरललनायान्ति मनसा
तपोभिर्दुष्प्रापामपि गिरिशसायुज्यपदवीं॥४॥

Transliteration:

tvadīyaṁ saundaryaṁ tuhina-giri-kanye tulayituṁ
kavīndrāḥ kalpante katham api viriñci-prabhṛtayaḥ |
yadālokautsukyād amara-lalanā yānti manasā
tapobhir duṣprāpām api giriśa-sāyujya-padavīm || 4 ||

Translation:
O Daughter of the Himalayas, even the greatest poets and Brahmā himself
struggle to match Your beauty.
Desiring a glimpse of You, the celestial maidens
aspire mentally to a union with You that even intense austerity rarely attains.

□

Sanskrit:
षष्ठिः सम्पत्तिः किञ्चिदपरमिष्टं तनुभृतां
न चेदेवं तावन्मणिमणितनुं त्वां न भजते।
स्मरं वर्णीं चान्द्रीं वहति भुवनैः वन्दितपदां
सुरेन्द्रानां दर्पं शमयति शरस्यैव निभृता॥५॥

Transliteration:
ṣaṣṭhiḥ sampattiḥ kiñcid aparam iṣṭaṁ tanubhṛtāṁ
na ced evaṁ tāvan maṇi-maṇi-tanuṁ tvāṁ na bhajate |
smaraṁ varṇīṁ cāndrīṁ vahati bhuvanaiḥ vandita-padāṁ
surendrāṇāṁ darpaṁ śamayati śarasyaiva nibhṛtā || 5 ||

Translation:
Even if one possesses all six types of wealth, something remains missing
unless they adore Your jewel-like body.
You bear Kāmadeva, Viṣṇu, and the Moon under Your feet—
silently, with just an arrow, You humble the pride of the gods.

□

Sanskrit:
तनुच्छायाभिस्ते तरुणतरिशुर्भिः प्रणतिभिः
अशेषं मोहेन सपदि परितापं च दधति।

सुधा स्यन्दं वाचा मधुरमधुरैर्भावति तया
गणानां पितुः किं नयनमणिमज्ज्योत्स्ना रचयति॥६॥

Transliteration:
tanu-cchāyābhis te taruṇa-tariśurbhiḥ praṇatibhiḥ
aśeṣaṁ mohena sapadi paritāpaṁ ca dadhati |
sudhā-syandaṁ vācā madhura-madhuraiḥ bhāvayati tayā
gaṇānāṁ pituḥ kiṁ nayana-maṇi-maj-jyotsnā racayati || 6 ||

Translation:
With the shadows of Your youthful glances cast on the devoted,
You immediately dissolve all illusion and suffering.
With nectar-sweet words, You stir hearts—
even Śiva, Lord of the Gaṇas, is bathed in the moonlight of Your gaze.

▯

Sanskrit:
क्वणत्काञ्चीदामा करिकलभकुम्भस्तननता
परिक्षीणामध्ये परिणतशरच्चन्द्रवदना।
धनुर्बाणान्पाशं सृणिमपि दधाना करतलैः
पुरस्तादास्तां नः पुरमथितुराहोपुरुषिका॥७॥

Transliteration:
kvaṇat-kāñcī-dāmā karikalabha-kumbha-stana-natā
parikṣīṇāmadhye pariṇata-śarat-candra-vadanā |
dhanur bāṇān pāśaṁ sṛṇim api dadhānā karatalaiḥ
purastād āstāṁ naḥ puramathitur āhopuruṣikā || 7 ||

Translation:
May She stand before us—
the consort of Śiva, destroyer of the cities—
adorned with a jingling girdle, breasts like elephant temples,
a slim waist, a face like the autumn moon,
holding bow, arrows, noose, and hook in Her hands.

▯

Sanskrit:
सुधामप्यास्वाद्य प्रतिभयजरामृत्युहरणं
विपद्यन्ते विश्वे विधिशतमुखादाः विवशतया।
स्मरं योनिं लक्ष्मीं त्रितयमिदमादौ तव मनः
स्थितं नैवातत्त्वं किमपि यदतिष्ठन्नपि शिवः॥८॥

Transliteration:
sudhām apy āsvādya pratibhaya-jarāmṛtyu-haraṇaṁ
vipadyante viśve vidhi-śata-mukhādāḥ vivaśatayā |
smaraṁ yoniṁ lakṣmīṁ tritayam idam ādau tava manaḥ
sthitaṁ naivātattvaṁ kim api yad atiṣṭhann api śivaḥ || 8 ||

Translation:
Even after tasting nectar that removes fear, old age, and death,
the worlds and their lords like Brahmā fall powerless.
Since You placed within Your heart Kāmadeva, the Yoni, and Lakṣmī,
even Śiva, though beyond all, abides in dependence on You.

□

Sanskrit:
धनुः पौष्पं मौर्वी मधुकरमयी पञ्चविशिखाः
वसन्तः सामन्तो मलयमरुदायोधनरथः।
चषेणुर्मे चैषाऽपरिणतशरः कोऽपि न भवेत्
तस्मान्नः स्मेरं त्वमुखमपि चक्षुष्मतां श्रियम्॥९॥

Transliteration:
dhanuḥ pauṣpaṁ maurvī madhukara-mayī pañca-viśikhāḥ
vasantaḥ sāmaṁto malaya-marud āyodhana-rathaḥ |
caṣeṇur me cai'ṣāpariṇata-śaraḥ ko'pi na bhavet
tasmān naḥ smeram tva-mukham api cakṣuṣmatāṁ śriyam || 9 ||

Translation:
His bow is of flowers, its string of fibers,
his arrows are bees, and Spring is his commander;
his chariot is the Malaya breeze.
Yet who can resist this immature Kāmadeva?

Let Your smiling face be the true treasure for our eyes.

▯

Sanskrit:
सुधासिन्धोर्मध्ये सुरविटपिवाटीपरिवृते
मणिद्वीपे निप्ये निखिलमणिमाणामृतमये।
श्रियोदन्यैर्देवैः सखलसुभगैरावृतमभूत्
स्मरारिः त्वां नत्वा स्ववपुषि निधायापरमपि॥१०॥

Transliteration:
sudhā-sindhor madhye sura-viṭapi-vāṭī-parivṛte
maṇi-dvīpe nitye nikhila-maṇi-māṇāmṛtamaye |
śriyodanyair devaiḥ sakala-subhagaiḥ āvṛtam abhūt
smarāriḥ tvāṁ natvā sva-vapuṣi nidhāyāparam api || 10 ||

Translation:
In the midst of the ocean of nectar, surrounded by divine trees,
stands an eternal island of gems, shining with immortal light.
There, with other radiant goddesses, dwells Śrī.
Śiva, conqueror of Kāmadeva, bows to You,
and unites with You, absorbing Your very essence.

11.

Sanskrit:
चतुःषष्ट्या तन्त्रैः सकलमतसन्मेलनमिलत्
स्मरारुण्यां लीलया विघटितानन्तपभुवाम्।
शिवः शक्त्या युक्तो यदि भवति शक्तः प्रभवितुं
न चेदेवं देवो न खलु कुशलः स्पन्दितुमपि॥११॥

Transliteration:
catuḥṣaṣṭyā tantraiḥ sakala-mata-sanmēlana-milat
smarāruṇyāṁ līlayā vighaṭitānanta-pabhubhām |
śivaḥ śaktyā yukto yadi bhavati śaktaḥ prabhavitum
na ced evaṁ devo na khalu kuśalaḥ spanditum api || 11 ||

Translation:
With sixty-four Tantras, the essence of all doctrines,

You, red with passion, playfully unfold infinite worlds.
Only when united with Shakti can Shiva act;
Otherwise, even the Divine cannot stir or act.

□

12.

Sanskrit:
अतस्त्वामाराध्यां हरिहरविरिञ्चादिभिरपि
प्रणन्तुं स्तोतुं वा कथमकृतपुण्यः प्रभवति।
अतः स त्वां दृष्ट्वा तनुयुगलरूपं तव यते
हरिः स्यात्त्वं रुद्रः स भवति सती त्वं च गिरिशः॥१२॥

Transliteration:
atas tvām ārādhyāṁ hari-hara-viriñcādibhir api
praṇantuṁ stotuṁ vā katham akṛta-puṇyaḥ prabhavati |
ataḥ sa tvāṁ dṛṣṭvā tanu-yugala-rūpaṁ tava yate
hariḥ syāt tvaṁ rudraḥ sa bhavati satī tvaṁ ca giriśaḥ || 12 ||

Translation:
Thus even Hari, Hara, and Brahmā worship you.
How can one without merit even bow or praise you?
Seeing your dual form, one becomes Vishnu, you become Rudra,
He becomes Sati, and you, O Goddess, become Giriśa.

□

13.

Sanskrit:
सरोरुहानां त्वां शरणमुपगत्वा कृतमला
नलिन्यां नीतायां नलिनदलगन्धं स्निहयति।
इति त्वद्वक्षोजावमृतरससाराऽऽभरणतः
अपाङ्गात्ते लीलाङ्गितिवशात्तर्प्यति सखा॥१३॥

Transliteration:
saroruhānāṁ tvāṁ śaraṇam upagatyā kṛta-malā
nalinyāṁ nītāyāṁ nalina-dala-gandhaṁ snihayati |
iti tvad-vakṣojāv amṛta-rasa-sārābharaṇataḥ

apāṅgāt te līlāṅgiti-vaśāt tarpyati sakhā || 13 ||

Translation:
Even the lotus flowers, once purified by taking refuge in you,
lose their fondness for ordinary lotus fragrance.
From your breasts adorned with the essence of nectar,
just one playful side glance suffices to satisfy the beloved.

▯

14.

Sanskrit:
तव स्तन्यं मन्ये धरणिधरकन्ये हृदयतः
पयःपारावारं परिवहति सारस्वतमिव।
दयावत्या दत्तं द्रवणमधुरं यत्कविता
वपुस्तत्तत्त्वेन प्रतिपदमतर्व्यग्गृणुते॥१४॥

Transliteration:
tava stanyaṁ manye dharaṇi-dhara-kanye hṛdayataḥ
payaḥ-pārāvāraṁ parivahati sārasvatam iva |
dayāvatyā dattaṁ dravaṇa-madhuraṁ yat kavitā
vapus tat tattvena pratipadaṁ atarvyag ṛṇute || 14 ||

Translation:
O daughter of the mountain, your milk flows
like an ocean of Sarasvat'īs wisdom from your heart.
Poetry given by your compassion, sweet and melting,
is embodied truth in every word it utters.

▯

15.

Sanskrit:
हरं लक्ष्मीपत्यं हरिणपारिपत्यस्य परतः
स्वपन्थानं सेवं स्तनमणिमनञ्जीरनिवहतः।
तवास्मिन् मानत्वं कलयति हरिणा लाघवयतः
समुन्मीलत्स्तन्यं सहरशमुपैतिं दृढमिति॥१५॥

Transliteration:
haraṁ lakṣmī-patyaṁ hariṇa-pāri-patyasya parataḥ
sva-panthānaṁ sevam stana-maṇi-mañjīra-nivahataḥ |
tavāsmin mānatvaṁ kalayati hariṇā lāghavayataḥ
samunmīlat stanyaṁ saharaśam upaiti dṛḍham iti || 15 ||

Translation:
Lakṣmī loves Hari, Pārvatī loves Hara,
he who worships your breast adorned with jeweled bells
gains honor even among the gods,
for your milk, welling forth, brings steadfast realization.

▯

16.

Sanskrit:
तव भ्रूलाताक्षेपजनितशिरोध्याकृतिपरं
शिरस्ते संयच्छत्यति महित तत्त्वं किमपि यत्।
निरालम्बं लक्ष्मीं धृतधरणिरूपां नयनयोर्
निलीनां यद्रूपं निखिलमपि धत्ते नयनता॥१६॥

Transliteration:
tava bhrū-lātākṣepa-janita-śiro-dhyākṛti-paraṁ
śiras te saṁyacchaty ati-mahita-tattvaṁ kim api yat |
nirālambaṁ lakṣmīṁ dhṛta-dharaṇi-rūpāṁ nayanayoḥ
nilīnāṁ yad rūpaṁ nikhilam api dhatte nayanatā || 16 ||

Translation:
Your eyebrow's movement reveals supreme truths,
and one who contemplates it bows the head in awe.
That unsupported Lakṣmī, in earthly form,
rests hidden in your eyes—eyes that create all vision.

▯

17.

Sanskrit:

विभक्तत्रैवर्ण्यं व्यतिकरितलीलाञ्चितमिव
त्रिरेखाभिः शून्यं त्रिभुवनमशेषं तव यशः।
क्वणत्काञ्चीदामा करिकलभकुम्भस्तननता
समुन्नेयात्कर्णोचितशिरसि पत्रं स्त्रिय इव॥१७॥

Transliteration:
vibhakta-traivarṇyaṁ vyatikarita-līlāñcitam iva
tri-rekhābhiḥ śūnyaṁ tribhuvanam aśeṣaṁ tava yaśaḥ |
kvaṇat-kāñcī-dāmā karikalabha-kumbha-stana-natā
samunnēyāt-karṇocita-śirasi patraṁ striya iva || 17 ||

Translation:
Your glory pervades the three worlds,
as the triple lines on your belly mark the sacred triad.
With jingling belt, elephant-round breasts,
you rise like a woman adorning her hair with a leaf.

□

18.

Sanskrit:
सुधासिन्धोर्मध्ये सुरविटपिवाटीपरिवृते
मणिद्वीपे नित्ये निखिलमणिमाणामृतमये।
श्रियोदन्यैर्देवैः सखलसुभगैरावृतमभूत्
स्मरारिः त्वां नत्वा स्ववपुषि निधायापरमपि॥१८॥

Transliteration:
sudhā-sindhor madhye sura-viṭapi-vāṭī-parivṛte
maṇi-dvīpe nitye nikhila-maṇi-māṇāmṛta-maye |
śriyodanyair devaiḥ sakala-subhagaiḥ āvṛtam abhūt
smarāriḥ tvāṁ natvā sva-vapuṣi nidhāyāparam api || 18 ||

Translation:
In the nectar ocean's midst, encircled by heavenly groves,
shines the eternal gem island, formed of immortal jewels.
There, with all divine beauties around, Śiva, slayer of Kāmadeva,
bows to you and merges your being into his own.

□

19.

Sanskrit:
त्वदीयं सौन्दर्यं तुहिनगिरिकन्ये तुलयितुं
कवीन्द्राः कल्पन्ते कथमपि विरिञ्चिप्रभृतयः।
यदालोकौत्सुक्यादमरललनायान्ति मनसा
तपोभिर्दुष्प्रापामपि गिरिसुते त्वां विजयते॥१९॥

Transliteration:
tvadīyaṁ saundaryaṁ tuhina-giri-kanye tulayituṁ
kavīndrāḥ kalpante katham api viriñci-prabhṛtayaḥ |
yadālokautsukyād amara-lalanā yānti manasā
tapobhir duṣprāpām api giri-sute tvāṁ vijayate || 19 ||

Translation:
O daughter of the Himālaya, even the wisest poets, even Brahmā, struggle to match your beauty in their thoughts.
Heavenly maidens yearn to behold you,
though you, O mountain-born, are reached only through great austerity.

□

20.

Sanskrit:
नरं वरिष्ठं नयनविषयं नापि च गतम्
सदापश्यन्त्यो योषण्यमितरसमानासमरुचिः।
स्वयं कृत्वा मौलिं तव कटकमौलिपरिचयः
शिरस्ते संरम्भं समजनित शीतांशुशकलः॥२०॥

Transliteration:
naraṁ varṣīyāṁsaṁ nayana-viṣayaṁ nāpi ca gatam
sadā paśyantyo yoṣaṇyam itarā-samānā-sama-ruciḥ |
svayaṁ kṛtvā mauliṁ tava kaṭaka-mauli-paricayaḥ
śiras te saṁrambhaṁ samajanita śītāṁśu-śakalaḥ || 20 ||

Translation:
You never look upon younger or handsomer men,
and other women see you as their equal in beauty.
When the crescent moon adorned your crown,
it trembled in awe of your splendor.

21.

Sanskrit:
हिमानी हन्तव्या हिमगिरिशिलाबन्धुकविता
तव स्तोतो ज्ञेयः कथमिव सतां भाषितपथः।
कलङ्कः कस्तूरीरजनगुणता योऽपि हरिते
न लक्ष्मीपात्रत्वं व्रजति पतति वर्णस्य भवतः॥२१॥

Transliteration:
himānī hantavyā hima-giri-śilā-bandhu-kavitā
tava stoto jñeyaḥ katham iva satāṁ bhāṣita-pathaḥ |
kalaṅkaḥ kastūrī-rajana-guṇatā yo'pi harite
na lakṣmī-pātratvaṁ vrajati patati varṇasya bhavataḥ || 21 ||

Translation:
What worth is cold poetry, like the icy stones of the Himalayas,
when one tries to praise You? Even the words of sages are not enough.
A blemish, even if fragrant like musk upon a leaf,
does not make that leaf worthy of the goddess of fortune.

▯

22.

Sanskrit:
कदाचित्कालिन्दीतटविपिनसङ्गीतकटरे
मृगानुभ्रान्तं स्वं रुधिरनिभरक्ताक्षमधुरम्।
तृणं तम्बूलं वा तदपि कवलेनाप्युपहृतं
सृणीयात्सन्देहं न हि चरितमिन्दीवरशयम्॥२२॥

Transliteration:

kadācit kālindī-taṭa-vipina-saṅgīta-kaṭare
mṛgānu-bhrāntaṁ svaṁ rudhira-nibha-raktākṣa-madhuram |
tṛṇaṁ tambūlaṁ vā tad api kavalenāpy upahṛtaṁ
sṛṇīyāt saṁdehaṁ na hi caritam indīvara-śayam || 22 ||

Translation:
If one day a deer, lost along the banks of the Yamunā,
with sweet eyes red as blood,
offers You a mere blade of grass or a betel leaf,
accept it without hesitation: even a small gift is noble when offered with devotion.

▯

23.

Sanskrit:
क्षणं जातं पश्यन्नवतनुसरोरुहं इव
स्त्रिया मूर्त्या मध्ये रमणमणिमञ्जीररचनः।
अधः पश्यन् शीर्षे निरुपमसरोरुहदृशः
तदाल्लेख्यं साध्यं किमपि न तव श्रीरहितम्॥२३॥

Transliteration:
kṣaṇaṁ jātaṁ paśyann avatanu-saroruhaṁ iva
striyā mūrtyā madhye ramaṇa-maṇi-mañjīra-racanaḥ |
adhaḥ paśyan śīrṣe nirupama-saroruha-dṛśaḥ
tad ālekhyaṁ sādhyaṁ kim api na tava śrī-rahitam || 23 ||

Translation:
One who glimpses for a moment the lotus that is You, in Your perfect feminine form,
adorned with jeweled anklets of love,
will see another incomparable lotus in Your gaze.
What can be painted without Your grace?

▯

24.

Sanskrit:

तवापादलम्बत्रितयमणिमञ्जीररणितं
चकोराणां तृष्टिः युगपदिव नक्तं दिवमपि।
महा-पद्माटव्यां मृदितमलिनीपुष्करभवः
श्रियं कृत्वा मन्दं सपदि विघटन्ते गगनयः॥२४॥

Transliteration:
tavāpāda-lamba-tritaya-maṇi-mañjīra-raṇitaṁ
cakorāṇāṁ tṛṣṭiḥ yugapad iva naktaṁ divam api |
mahā-padma-āṭavyāṁ mṛdita-malinī-puṣkara-bhavaḥ
śriyaṁ kṛtvā mandaṁ sapadi vighaṭante gaganayaḥ || 24 ||

Translation:
The sound of Your three anklets resounds gently,
like the yearning of the cakora bird for the moon, day and night.
When Your feet tread the forest of great lotuses,
even the clouds scatter, unable to match Your beauty.

▯

25.

Sanskrit:
नमः त्वं काञ्चनाङ्ग्यै कमलदलनेत्राय दयिते
शिरः पुष्णात्येते तव चरणपङ्केरुहरुहं।
विधत्तां यस्तावज्जननि लघुलीलाञ्चलधृतिं
नृणां चित्ते लक्ष्मीं निवसतु चिरं पुण्यगुणया॥२५॥

Transliteration:
namaḥ tvaṁ kāñcanāṅgyai kamala-dala-netrāya dayite
śiraḥ puṣṇāty ete tava caraṇa-paṅkeruha-ruhaṁ |
vidhattāṁ yas tāvaj janani laghu-līlāñcala-dhṛtiṁ
nṛṇāṁ citte lakṣmīṁ nivasatu ciraṁ puṇya-guṇayā || 25 ||

Translation:
Homage to You, with a golden body and eyes like lotus petals,
whose lotus feet bless every bowed head.
O Mother, let the light touch of Your garment's hem
cause Lakṣmī to dwell long in the hearts of those who praise You with devotion.

▯

26.

Translation:
Those who worship Your radiant form,
like the rising sun in the garden of poets 'hearts,
surpass even the Vedic paths lauded by Brahmā;
for him too, the supreme fruit is to meditate upon Your name.

▯

27.

Translation:
You bestow the supreme poetic art upon those
who offer You their devotion with sincere affection.
These sages, who praise You in the divine assemblies,
honor Your beauty, adorned with the garland of grace
and the gentle charm of deer-like eyes.

▯

28.

Translation:
In the ocean of nectar, surrounded by heavenly groves,
on a jeweled island where the sages of the Upaniṣads dwell,
the great yogis rest in Your Supreme Consciousness,
full of eternal bliss and overflowing divine power.

▯

29.

Translation:
Your abode radiates supreme wealth, unreachable even to yogis,
yet by divine command, You enter the hearts of the faithful.
O Mother, when You gaze upon beings with compassion,
You manifest visibly, united with Śiva.

▯

30.

Translation:
Whether through japa, hymns, mantra, or meditation,
whatever discipline leads the devotee to You,
O glorious Mother, all praises aim toward You.
But none of these is subtler or more sublime than Your very essence.

▯

31.

Translation:
O Mother, those who do not meditate upon You—
Śiva's eternal consort, remover of birth and death—
and worship only other paths,
miss this precious way to liberation,
which, once neglected, is not easily regained.

▯

32.

Translation:
You are the radiant city-island dissolving
the inner darkness of ignorance,
the nectar stream awakening the dull,
the wish-fulfilling gem for the poor,
and, for those drowning in the ocean of rebirth,
the saving tusk of Viṣṇu's Boar form.

▯

33.

Translation:
Even for a moment, if You are pleased,

O Yogini, O Lady, grace pours down like rain.
Tell me, what fruit can destiny or knowledge give
that compares to Your blessing?
Neither power nor learning can gain
what devotion to You alone reveals.

▯

34.

Translation:
O Mother, who appeared as Kātyāyanī on the Golden Mountain,
though I've recited mantras,
I've gained not the slightest benefit.
I am abandoned, helpless—
there is no one else.
O Mother, behold me in this pitiful state
as I fall into saṁsāra—guide me!

▯

35.

Translation:
O Śive (Divine Mother),
true worship of the three deities born of the guṇas
is in fact the worship of Your feet.
Yet only a few, by great merit, realize this truth.
You never forsake anyone—
so how could You abandon me now?

▯

36.

Translation:
O Mother, Your beauty overwhelms all beings,
making them feel as beloved children to You.
Yet even Viṣṇu (Śauri), cleansed of all impurities
by Your steady gaze,

remains bound to You in deep affection,
enchanted by the sweetness of union.

▯

37.

Translation:
If the god of love, blind and without sight,
is struck by Your arrows and lies upon a coiled serpent,
what of my heart—fragile as a leaf in the wind?
Even if Your beauty is formless and unseen,
it stirs within me as a living presence.

▯

38.

Translation:
Even the nectar of immortality,
kept under Indra's sacred tree,
is less desired than Your autumn flower-bed,
where Śiva forever rests with You, O mighty Śakti.
This vision that inspires poets and sages
shines for me as a reflection of Your heart.

▯

39.

Translation:
She is pure as the autumn moonlight,
with the moon woven in her hair,
holding a book, a rosary,
the gestures of gift and protection.
How could devotees not taste the supreme sweetness—
richer than honey, milk, and grapes—
just by bowing once to Her?

▯

40.

Translation:
In the realm of poets, Your speech is inspiration,
sweet like distilled nectar,
droplets of ambrosia from Your lips enchanting the soul.
May this regal beauty of Your eyebrows,
surpassing even Sarasvat'īs words,
reign over my thoughts as sovereign.

41.
Sanskrit:
तवापर्णे कर्णे झणझणितनूपूररचिता
नदीनां वृन्दानां ननु विलयनाय त्रिभुवनम्।
नखानामुद्योतैर्नवनवदलश्रीतरणये
नवीनं पाटालं नवसहस्रसंख्या नयनया॥ ४१॥

Transliteration:
Tavāparṇe karṇe jhaṇa-jhaṇita-nūpūra-racitā
Nadīnāṁ vṛndānāṁ nanu vilayanāya tribhuvanam |
Nakhānām udyotair nava-navadala-śrī-taraṇaye
Navīnaṁ pāṭālaṁ nava-sahasra-saṁkhyā nayanayā || 41 ||

Translation:
O daughter of Himālaya, the tinkling of Your anklets
resounds like the merging of rivers across the three worlds.
The radiance of Your nails competes with the freshness of lotus buds,
and Your eyes, countless in number, open new subterranean realms of beauty.

▯

42.
Sanskrit:
नमः त्वं बालेन्दुं चपलधरया चारुतरया
स्मरं स्मारं भूषं मदनरिपुणा नाऽभिनयतः।

स्फुरन् मीनाभ्यां त्वं सहरिदयभूषा शुभकरी
नखाग्रच्छायाभिर्नतितमसमाराध्यवपुषः॥ ४२॥

Transliteration:
Namaḥ tvaṁ bālenduṁ capala-dharayā cārutarayā
Smaraṁ smāraṁ bhūṣaṁ madana-ripuṇā nābhinayataḥ |
Sphuran mīnādhyāṁ tvaṁ saharidaya-bhūṣā śubha-karī
Nakhāgra-chāyābhir natita-masam ārādhya-vapuṣaḥ || 42 ||

Translation:
Salutations to You, who wear the crescent moon and smile with graceful playfulness.
You are the living ornament of the god of love, even as the bride of his enemy, Śiva.
With eyes like darting fish and a heart adorned with benevolence, the shadows of Your nails dispel the darkness of those who adore You.

▯

43.
Sanskrit:
गते कर्णाभ्यर्णं गरुत इव पक्ष्मण्युबलम्
स्फुरल्लोचालक्ष्मीररुणधवलश्यामलरुचः।
नदः सूर्यासङ्गादणुतर इवाभाति तव यं
कदाचिद्वर्णानां व्यवहारनिबन्धं कलयति॥ ४३॥

Transliteration:
Gate karṇābhy-arṇaṁ garuta iva pakṣmaṇyu-balam
Sphurallochā-lakṣmīr aruṇa-dhavala-śyāmala-rucaḥ |
Nadaḥ sūryā-saṅgād aṇutara ivābhāti tava yaṁ
Kadācit varṇānāṁ vyavahāra-nibandhaṁ kalayati || 43 ||

Translation:
When the rays of Your eyes, glowing red, white, and blue,
move toward the ears, they resemble Garuḍa's wings in flight.
This stream of color, touched by sunlight, may seem small—
but it at times becomes the very origin of speech.

□

44.
Sanskrit:
दृशा दृष्टिं दोषात् गरुड इव दोषाय भुवनं
हरिष्यन्तं तेयं रसभरनमत्तं सृजति तम्।
सरागं सत्वानं शमितकिलबिखं सन्मनसां
वचः पुष्पं संहृत्य स्फुरति भवतां वर्णरुचिभिः॥ ४४॥

Transliteration:
Dṛśā dṛṣṭiṁ doṣāt garuḍa iva doṣāya bhuvanaṁ
Hariṣyantaṁ teyaṁ rasa-bhara-namattaṁ sṛjati tam |
Sarāgaṁ satvānaṁ śamita-kila-bikhaṁ sanmanasāṁ
Vacaḥ puṣpaṁ saṁhṛtya sphurati bhavatāṁ varṇa-rucibhiḥ || 44 ||

Translation:
Your gaze, when turned in wrath, can destroy the world like Garuḍa a serpent.
But when sweet and full of bliss, it generates deep love.
It pacifies the minds of the pure with grace and compassion,
and like gathered flower-words, gives rise to sacred sound and color.

□

45.
Sanskrit:
शिवे श्रृंगारार्द्रा तदितरजनाविस्मयकरी
स्मरः स्मर्तव्यः शमितभवदर्पं भवतु मे।
मनः शिष्यं पश्यन मदनयति मन्मथस्य स तु
स्त्रियां भावः सम्यक् किल नयति सौभाग्यजनकः॥ ४५॥

Transliteration:
Śive śṛṅgārārdraā tad-itara-janāvismaya-karī
Smaraḥ smartavyaḥ śamita-bhava-darpaṁ bhavatu me |
Manaḥ śiṣyaṁ paśyan madanayati manmathasya sa tu
Striyāṁ bhāvaḥ samyak kila nayati saubhāgya-janakaḥ || 45 ||

Translation:
O Śivā, tender in love and wondrous to Your devotees,
may the God of Love, whose pride You subdued, guide my heart.
Seeing my mind as his disciple,
may he lead me into union with You, source of all beauty.

46.
Sanskrit:
द्विषां बद्धः क्रोधं दहनकृणुते किं न हरिणी
शपं शक्रं बन्धं भ्रमयति फणिन्यापि चटुला।
अपस्मारं दृष्ट्वा सपदि सुरसंधानधिपतिं
त्वदीयं सौन्दर्यं जगदपि विमोहं तनुत इदम्॥ ४६॥

Transliteration:
Dviṣāṁ baddhaḥ krodhaṁ dahana-kṛṇute kiṁ na hariṇī
Śapaṁ śakraṁ bandhaṁ bhramayati phaṇinyāpi caṭulā |
Apasmāraṁ dṛṣṭvā sapadi sura-saṁdhāna-dhipatiṁ
Tvadīyaṁ saundaryaṁ jagad api vimoham tanuta idam || 46 ||

Translation:
If even a deer can arouse anger in enemies,
if a flash of lightning can bind, and a small snake disorient,
then surely Your beauty, O Goddess, once glimpsed,
can instantly bewilder even the lord of the gods.

▯

47.
Sanskrit:
विशुद्धौ ते शुद्धं विदधति यशोऽधिकमपि
स्तनाभ्यां नाभ्यां हिमगिरिसुते नापहरणम्।
इयं कन्ये तन्त्रीनिकरयुगलाक्षेपसरणिः
परं ते सन्देहं हरतु शरदिन्दोरिव तनुः॥ ४७॥

Transliteration:
Viśuddhau te śuddhaṁ vidadhati yaśo'dhikam api
Stanābhyāṁ nābhyāṁ himagiri-sute nāpaharaṇam |

Iyaṁ kanye tantrī-nikara-yugala-ākṣepa-saraṇiḥ
Paraṁ te sandehaṁ haratu śarad-indor iva tanuḥ || 47 ||

Translation:
O daughter of Himālaya, the purity in Your Viśuddha chakra
is exalted by the glory of Your breasts and navel.
This fine line that runs across Your form, like a string of veena wires,
may it dispel all doubt, as does the autumn moonlight.

▯

48.
Sanskrit:
नवीनं कन्दर्पं नयनकृतनैवेद्यरुचिरं
कदाचित्सम्पश्यन् कुशलनिलयं वा नरपतिः।
शशङ्के तद्भावं भवति सुखिनो वाञ्छितफलं
मनो मे तान्यं ते तनुभुवन सौन्दर्यसरणेः॥ ४८॥

Transliteration:
Navīnaṁ kandarpaṁ nayana-kṛta-naivedya-ruciraṁ
Kadācit sampaśyan kuśala-nilayaṁ vā narapatiḥ |
Śaśaṅke tad-bhāvaṁ bhavati sukhino vāñchita-phalaṁ
Mano me tānyaṁ te tanu-bhuvana saundarya-saraṇeḥ || 48 ||

Translation:
If a king were to glimpse, even once, the beauty of Your body—
a fresh offering fit for a new Kāmadeva—
he would be drawn into longing and attain his desired joy.
May my mind follow this path of Your embodied beauty.

▯

49.
Sanskrit:
शरज्ज्योत्स्नाशुद्धां शशियुतजटाजूटमुकुटां
वरेण्यां भक्तिं मे विमलमपि सन्तु त्रिजगति।
चिरं त्वामाराध्यां सखिजना रसानन्दसरणिं
विधत्ते मन्दस्मेरविकसितवदनां शशिमुखीम्॥ ४९॥

Transliteration:
Śarat-jyotsnā-śuddhāṁ śaśiyuta-jaṭā-jūṭa-mukuṭāṁ
Vareṇyāṁ bhaktiṁ me vimalam api santu trijagati |
Ciraṁ tvām ārādhyāṁ sakhijanā rasānanda-saraṇiṁ
Vidhatte manda-smera-vikasita-vadanāṁ śaśi-mukhīm || 49 ||

Translation:
May I offer pure devotion to You,
who shine with the clarity of the autumn moon,
wearing the crescent in Your matted hair.
Long worshiped by companions,
You are a path of joy and bliss,
Your face blooming with a gentle smile, moon-like and serene.

▯

50.
Sanskrit:
रुचिः प्राप्तं भूम्ना रविसहचरैरर्चितपदां
तथाप्येके नित्रां धृतरुचिरमालालसितया।
तदीयं सौन्दर्यं जगदपि मनोहारि कुहकं
मनो मे बन्धाय प्रकटयतु नः सन्निधिमपि॥ ५०॥

Transliteration:
Rucih prāptaṁ bhūmnā ravi-sahacarair arcita-padāṁ
Tathāpy eke nitrāṁ dhṛta-rucira-mālā-lasitayā |
Tadīyaṁ saundaryaṁ jagad api manohāri kuhakaṁ
Mano me bandhāya prakaṭayatu naḥ sannidhim api || 50 ||

Translation:
Though Your radiance is worshipped by the sun and planets,
only a few glimpse Your form adorned with radiant garlands.
Yet Your beauty enchants the entire universe—
may it bind my mind and reveal itself fully to me.

51.
Sanskrit:

अरालैः स्वाभाव्यादलिकुलभसृङ्गाभिरुचिभिः
वशिन्या दोषेण स्फुटतरफणात् मणिविभूतिः।
अनवाप्तं यश्च स्फुटमुपचितं भाति तदिदं
विदध्यादाऽनन्दं तव वदनसौन्दर्यशशिनः॥ ५१॥

Transliteration:
Arālaiḥ svābhāvyād alikula-bhasaṛṅgābhir ucibhiḥ
Vaśinyā doṣeṇa sphuṭatara-phaṇāt maṇi-vibhūtiḥ |
Anavāptaṁ yaś ca sphuṭam upacitaṁ bhāti tad idaṁ
Vidadhyād ānandaṁ tava vadana-saundarya-śaśinaḥ || 51 ||

Translation:
The natural curves of Your eyebrows, like the tips of a bee's antennae,
bestow upon You the power of Vaśinī,
enhancing the brilliance of the gem on Your radiant forehead.
May this perfect beauty bring bliss,
like the shining moon of Your divine face.

▯

52.
Sanskrit:
तवापर्णे कर्णे झणझणितकाञ्चीकलकलं
निनादं पुण्यानाṁ नवशशिमयूखोपमृतम्।
सहस्त्रारं चक्रं स्फुटघटितसन्धानविकसत्
सुधास्त्रावंत्याख्यां शिशिरमुपचारा युगपदे॥ ५२॥

Transliteration:
Tavāparṇe karṇe jhaṇa-jhaṇita-kāñcī-kalakalaṁ
Ninādaṁ puṇyānāṁ nava-śaśi-mayūkha-upamṛtam |
Sahasrāraṁ cakraṁ sphuṭa-ghaṭita-sandhāna-vikasat
Sudhā-srāvanty-ākhyāṁ śiśiram upacārā yugapade || 52 ||

Translation:
O Aparnā, the tinkling of Your waist-bells,
ringing near Your ears like a sweet melody,
is like nectar from new moonbeams savored by the pure.

It opens the Sahasrāra chakra,
from which flows the cool ambrosia of healing grace.

□

53.
Sanskrit:
तव स्नेहे धत्ते मम मनसि दत्त्वं च सुखिनां
विलासाश्चापाङ्गैः सकलजगतां मोहनवशात्।
सुधासिन्धुस्त्वं च ह्रद इव मनोहारिणि शिवे
सदाऽनन्दः क्रीडा नतजनरतेः सन्ततिमपि॥ ५३॥

Transliteration:
Tava snehe dhatte mama manasi dattvaṁ ca sukhināṁ
Vilāsāś cāpāṅgaiḥ sakala-jagatāṁ mohana-vaśāt |
Sudhā-sindhus tvaṁ ca hrada iva manohāriṇi śive
Sadānandaḥ krīḍā nata-jana-rateḥ santatim api || 53 ||

Translation:
Your love places within my mind
the fullness of joy known by the truly blessed.
With sidelong glances You enchant the whole world—
O delightful Śivā, You are a nectar-ocean,
a playful lake of bliss for those who bow before You.

□

54.
Sanskrit:
मनोबुद्ध्यहंकारचित्तनिनश्चानवस्थितं
सुराणां मर्त्यानां गतिगमविहीनं च मनसः।
त्वदीयं सौन्दर्यं किलिकलयते चेतसि कृतं
सुखं मे भक्तिस्ते त्वयि च सततं भावयतु माम्॥ ५४॥

Transliteration:
Mano-buddhyahaṅkāra-citta-ninaś cānavasthitaṁ
Surāṇāṁ martyānāṁ gati-gama-vihīnaṁ ca manasaḥ |
Tvadīyaṁ saundaryaṁ kilikalayate cetasi kṛtaṁ
Sukhaṁ me bhaktis te tvayi ca satataṁ bhāvayatu mām || 54 ||

Translation:
The mind, intellect, ego, and memory—
unstable in gods and humans alike—
lack the means to grasp the path or goal of life.
Yet Your beauty enchants them all.
May my devotion to You be constant,
and may it immerse me in Your presence.

□

55.
Sanskrit:
कदाचित्ते मातः किलकिलितभाषाविलसितैः
विलासैः कुर्वन्त्याः सुखसरणिमध्यापगमने।
मनो मे कालिन्दी-रसचपलता-यामलतया
त्वदङ्घ्रिद्वन्द्वाभ्यां गुरुतरगुणा स्यादुपगमः॥ ५५॥

Transliteration:
Kadācitte mātaḥ kilakilita-bhāṣā-vilasitaiḥ
Vilāsaiḥ kurvantyāḥ sukha-saraṇi-madhyāpagamane |
Mano me kālindī-rasa-capalatā-yāmalatayā
Tvad-aṅghri-dvandvābhyāṁ gurutara-guṇā syād upagamaḥ || 55 ||

Translation:
O Mother, if ever, with sweet words and graceful play,
You flow along the stream of joy,
may my mind—fickle like the Yamun'ās current—
be stilled and come to rest
at the twin feet of Your supreme virtues.

□

56.
Sanskrit:
नरं वरं वर्षं नयननवसंवादरुचिभिः
वशीनं वै शीते वपुषि मृगशीर्षेण नयना।
तवैषे भूयिष्ठं श्रुतिमुखरवाभिस्तु सुतरां

सखीसा सन्नद्धः कवय इव काव्यानि रचयेत्॥ ५६॥

Transliteration:
Naraṁ varaṁ varṣaṁ nayana-nava-saṁvāda-rucibhiḥ
Vaśīnaṁ vai śīte vapuṣi mṛga-śīrṣeṇa nayanā |
Tavaiṣe bhūyiṣṭhaṁ śruti-mukha-ravābhis tu sutarāṁ
Sakhīsā sannaddhaḥ kavaya iva kāvyāni racayet || 56 ||

Translation:
With fresh, silent dialogue from Your eyes,
You charm the noblest of men,
rendering them docile as deer in winter's season.
He who is joined with Your melodious voice
becomes like a poet, composing inspired verse.

□

57.
Sanskrit:
त्वदन्यः पाणिभ्यां अभयवरदो देव न मृषा
न यद्वा हस्तैर्वामोऽप्यनुभवननैकं न यमिनाम्।
सरांळं तं दृष्ट्वा तव नवरसास्वादतरले
कृपाणं हस्ताभ्यां सुभगतरसं वेत्ति सुधियः॥ ५७॥

Transliteration:
Tvadanyaḥ pāṇibhyām abhayavarado deva na mṛṣā
Na yadvā hastair vāmopy anubhavana-naikaṁ na yamināṁ |
Sarāḷaṁ taṁ dṛṣṭvā tava nava-rasāsvāda-tarale
Kṛpāṇaṁ hastābhyāṁ subhaga-tarasaṁ vetti sudhiyaḥ || 57 ||

Translation:
No god but You truly grants fearlessness and boon with both hands.
Though others raise theirs, they offer not the lived experience sought by yogis.
Seeing the graceful curve of Your hands,
the wise recognize in them
the most delightful essence of spiritual nectar.

▯

58.
Sanskrit:
नमस्तेस्तु नान्ते जगत इह पशूनां पशुपतेः
स्मरं स्मारं वह्निं विमथितमखं भस्मसहजान्।
कपालं सञ्चिन्वन्नकुलिशविषाणैकविमुखैः
शिरस्त्वन्दे वन्द्यं शिवभवति शेषैरपि सदा॥ ५८॥

Transliteration:
Namastes tu nānte jagata iha paśūnāṁ paśupateḥ
Smaraṁ smāraṁ vahniṁ vimathita-makhaṁ bhasma-sahajān |
Kapālaṁ sañcinvan nakuliśa-viṣāṇaika-vimukhaiḥ
Śiras tvam de vandyaṁ śiva bhavati śeṣair api sadā || 58 ||

Translation:
All bow to You, O Mother, even Paśupati, Lord of beings.
He who burned Kāma, quenched the sacrificial fire, and smeared himself with ash—
who gathers skulls and turns from celestial treasures—
even he always honors Your head,
knowing it surpasses all others.

▯

59.
Sanskrit:
तव स्तोत्रं नेत्रत्रितयगुणितं तां मनुशिवां
यदञ्जनं विद्या वलयितमणिं कण्ठलसितम्।
शिवस्यास्यं सुन्दं जपतु जननी मङ्गलमयं
नवीनं तं गानं सकलभुवनस्फारितमहः॥ ५९॥

Transliteration:
Tava stotraṁ netra-tritaya-guṇitaṁ tāṁ manu-śivāṁ
Yad añjanaṁ vidyā valayita-maṇiṁ kaṇṭha-lasitam |
Śivasyāsyaṁ sundaṁ japatu jananī maṅgala-mayaṁ
Navīnaṁ taṁ gānaṁ sakala-bhuvana-sphārita-mahaḥ || 59 ||

Translation:
Your hymn, born of the power of Your three eyes,
is like sacred kajal—
a gem encircled with mantra, adorning Śiva's throat.
May the Mother recite that auspicious song,
a new melody spreading glory through all worlds.

□

60.
Sanskrit:
सदासल्लापानां स्फुटपदकलापैः सुमधुरैः
विचित्रैस्ते चित्रैः कवितविषयैः स्रग्धिगुणितैः।
वाचां देवि त्वं स्फुरसि भवसिन्धौ नवसुधा
सरोजे ते वाण्याः स्फुरतु सुभगं रागमधुरा॥ ६०॥

Transliteration:
Sadā-sallāpānāṁ sphuṭa-pada-kalāpaiḥ su-madhuraiḥ
Vicitrais te citraiḥ kavita-viṣayaiḥ sragdhi-guṇitaiḥ |
Vācāṁ devi tvaṁ sphurasi bhava-sindhau nava-sudhā
Saroje te vāṇyāḥ sphuratu subhagaṁ rāga-madhurā || 60 ||

Translation:
O Goddess, with clear, melodious words,
woven like garlands with poetic meanings,
You shine as fresh nectar
upon the ocean of worldly existence.
May the speech arising from Your lotus-throat
blossom sweetly with beauty and melody.

61.
Sanskrit:
तवापर्णे कर्णे जपझणिति सञ्ज्ञातगुणिता
विवृत्य स्वं धाम प्रकटनमिवाघूर्णयति तत्।
चकस्ते वाञ्छासंसदि चिरमसौ नैव पुरतः
कदा वारं वारं किमपि कथयन्तीव जपसा॥ ६१॥

Transliteration:

Tavāparṇe karṇe japa-jhaṇiti sañjāta-guṇitā
Vivṛtya svaṁ dhāma prakaṭanam ivāghūrṇayati tat |
Cakaste vāñchā-saṁsadi ciram asau naiva purataḥ
Kadā vāraṁ vāraṁ kim api kathayantīva japasā || 61 ||

Translation:
O Parṇe (Durgā), the subtle japa-sound near Your ear seems to stir the universe, as if to reveal Your true nature. She does not appear immediately to fulfill the seeker's desires, but seems to whisper something again and again through silent mantra.

▯

62.
Sanskrit:
नलिन्याः अन्तःकिन्चिदिव मनोहारि निगलितं
कवीनां सन्दर्भे किमपि च महादेव्युपहरम्।
स्मरं स्मरं वाचं मधुरिमपरा माधुरिमयीं
प्रवृत्तिं सञ्जन्यां पुनरपि पुनः सेतुयति यतः॥ ६२॥

Transliteration:
Nalinyāḥ antaḥ kiñcid iva manohāri nigalitaṁ
Kavīnāṁ sandarbhe kim api ca mahā-devy-upaharam |
Smaraṁ smaraṁ vācaṁ madhurima-parā mādhurimayīṁ
Pravṛttiṁ sañjanyāṁ punar api punaḥ setuyati yataḥ || 62 ||

Translation:
As if a sweet mystery were hidden inside a lotus 'heart,
so is Your speech, O Supreme Goddess—gift to the poets.
When recalled, that voice steeped in supreme sweetness
inspires expression again and again in the hearts of men.

▯

63.
Sanskrit:
नभः स्पर्शं लक्ष्मीः चतुरभुजि संज्ञे सुमनसां
मनोबुद्धिप्रज्ञाः प्रशमयितुमीहेदिव सुखम्।

कथं तां त्वां वन्दे सकलभुवनानामधिपतीं
स्वयंज्योतिर्बिम्बं कमलनयनामम्ब मनुना॥ ६३॥

Transliteration:
Nabhaḥ sparśaṁ lakṣmīḥ caturabhuji sañjñe sumanasāṁ
Mano-buddhi-prajñāḥ praśamayitum īhe diva sukham |
Kathaṁ tāṁ tvāṁ vande sakala-bhuvanānām adhipatīṁ
Svayaṁ-jyotir-bimbaṁ kamala-nayanām amba manunā || 63 ||

Translation:
Lakṣmī, She who touches the heavens with four arms,
is worshipped by the pure to calm mind, intellect, and wisdom.
How could I not honor You, O Mother—Sovereign of all worlds,
Self-luminous One, with lotus-like eyes?

▯

64.
Sanskrit:
सुधासिन्धोर्मध्ये सुरविटपिवाटीपरिवृते
मणिद्वीपे नीपोपवनवति चिन्तामणिगृहे।
शिवाकारे मञ्चे परमशिवपारम्परवसतां
भजंस्त्वां चिन्तामणिगुणनिबद्धाक्षवलयम्॥ ६४॥

Transliteration:
Sudhā-sindhor madhye sura-viṭapi-vāṭī-parivṛte
Maṇi-dvīpe nīpōpavana-vati cintāmaṇi-gṛhe |
Śivākāre mañce paramaśiva-pārampara-vasatāṁ
Bhajaṁs tvāṁ cintāmaṇi-guṇa-nibaddhākṣa-valayam || 64 ||

Translation:
In the nectar ocean's midst, encircled by celestial groves,
lies the gem island, adorned with sacred trees,
where stands Your jeweled mansion,
and You rest on Śiva's throne, adorned with a rosary of wish-fulfilling gems.

▯

65.
Sanskrit:
सकृच्छिन्तां मन्मे तव चरणपङ्केरुहु-रुचिं
भवद्व्याधिः शान्त्यै न च चिरमिह सौख्याय भजते।
नमस्ते स्त्रीकायै नितरमभयायै च मम ते
दृशां दत्तं रूपं दुरितहरणं त्वं तु शिवदृशः॥ ६५॥

Transliteration:
Sakṛc-chintāṁ manme tava caraṇa-paṅkeruha-ruciṁ
Bhavad-vyādhiḥ śāntyai na ca ciram iha saukhyāya bhajate |
Namaste strīkāyai nitaram abhayāyai ca mama te
Dṛśāṁ dattaṁ rūpaṁ durita-haraṇaṁ tvaṁ tu śiva-dṛśaḥ || 65 ||

Translation:
Even a single thought of Your lotus feet
soothes the affliction of birth, bringing true joy.
I bow to You, Feminine Form—Supreme Giver of Fearlessness.
The beauty You reveal to the eyes
is Śiva's own gaze that destroys all misfortune.

□

66.
Sanskrit:
त्वदन्यः पाणिभ्यां अभयवरदो दैवतगणः
त्वमेकानैवासी प्रणयसमये कर्मचतुरः।
न च क्रूरं त्वत्तः किमपि करुणायाः कुबुधयः
कदाऽवा लोकेऽस्मिन् कथयतु कदाऽवा नवसति॥ ६६॥

Transliteration:
Tvad anyaḥ pāṇibhyām abhaya-varado daivata-gaṇaḥ
Tvam ekānaivāsī praṇaya-samaye karma-caturaḥ |
Na ca krūraṁ tvattaḥ kim api karuṇāyāḥ kubudhayaḥ
Kadā vā loke'smin kathayatu kadā vā nivasati || 66 ||

Translation:
All other gods grant protection and blessings with two hands,
but You alone, with four, act skillfully in love.

Yet fools speak of cruelty in You...
Tell me, when has the world ever known compassion greater than Yours?

▯

67.
Sanskrit:
कषायं वश्यत्वं श्रियमति सघाभाग्यरसिकां
वशीकर्तुं शक्रं कधमपि च साम्राज्यचटुलां।
तव द्वारे प्राप्ते पतिवरसमाराध्यगिरिणा
चतुःषष्ट्या तन्त्रैः सकलमतिसंधाय भवती॥ ६७॥

Transliteration:
Kaṣāyaṁ vaśyatvaṁ śriyam ati-saghā-bhāgya-rasikāṁ
Vaśīkartum śakraṁ kadham api ca sāmrājya-caṭulām |
Tava dvāre prāpte pativara-samārādhya-giriṇā
Catuḥṣaṣṭyā tantraiḥ sakala-mati-sandhāya bhavatī || 67 ||

Translation:
To attain control, wealth, and dominion over fate—
even to conquer Indra and the kingdom of heaven—
Himālaya, the wise one, worshipped You as the perfect bride,
and You, through sixty-four tantras, now shape all minds.

▯

68.
Sanskrit:
शिवः शक्त्या युक्तो यदि भवति शक्तः प्रभवितुं
न चेदेवं देवो न खलु कुशलः स्पन्दितुमपि।
अतस्त्वां आराध्यां हरिहरविरिञ्चादिभिरपि
प्रणन्तुं स्तोतुं वा कथमकृतपुण्यः प्रभवति॥ ६८॥

Transliteration:
Śivaḥ śaktyā yukto yadi bhavati śaktaḥ prabhavitum
Na ced evaṁ devo na khalu kuśalaḥ spanditum api |
Atas tvāṁ ārādhyāṁ hari-hara-viriñcādibhir api
Praṇantuṁ stotuṁ vā katham akṛta-puṇyaḥ prabhavati || 68 ||

Translation:
Only when united with Śakti does Śiva gain power to create.
Without Her, even the god cannot stir or act.
Thus You are worshipped by Viṣṇu, Śiva, and Brahmā—
how could anyone lacking merit dare to praise You?

▯

69.
Sanskrit:
त्वया हृत्वा वामं वपुः कुचलतां पञ्चतुलया
सुधा सिन्दोः मध्ये सुरविटपिवाटीपरिवृते।
मणिद्वीपे निपोपवनवति चिन्तामणिगृहे
शिवाकारं मञ्चं विरचयति चित्ते सुजनतः॥ ६९॥

Transliteration:
Tvayā hṛtvā vāmaṁ vapuḥ ku-calatāṁ pañca-tulayā
Sudhā-sindhoḥ madhye sura-viṭapi-vāṭī-parivṛte |
Maṇi-dvīpe nipopavanavati cintāmaṇi-gṛhe
Śivākāraṁ mañcaṁ viracayati citte sujanataḥ || 69 ||

Translation:
Taking Śiva's left half and purifying it with five golden virtues,
You dwell in the nectar-ocean's center, amidst divine gardens.
On the gem-island, in the wish-fulfilling palace,
the pure envision You seated on a throne shaped like Śiva Himself.

▯

70.
Sanskrit:
कदाचित्ताल्लोकं क्षणमपि कथं सन्निधवती
शिवः स्वात्मानं तव यदि सुखानामुपनयेत्।
दृशा मुञ्चन्त्येनं खलु भवसृजां लक्ष्यविभवं
तवास्यायासिद्धिं हरमहिषि सद्यो विनयति॥ ७०॥

Transliteration:
Kadā-cittāl lokaṁ kṣaṇam api kathaṁ sannidhavatī

Śivaḥ svātmānaṁ tava yadi sukhānām upanayet |
Dṛśā muñcanty enaṁ khalu bhava-sṛjāṁ lakṣya-vibhavaṁ
Tavāsyāyāsiddhiṁ hara-mahiṣi sadyo vinayati || 70 ||

Translation:
If ever Śiva offers Himself to You for even a moment,
O Consort of Hara, to enjoy Your bliss,
Your gaze alone dissolves the powers of worldly creators,
and humbles their efforts in an instant.

71.
Sanskrit:
धनुः पुण्याऽपाणां तपमपि तनोः पावनगुणं
कियत्कारं युक्तं किमु फलमपि क्लेशहतये।
अमुष्य त्वन्नेत्रं यदुयुगलमृक्शणदृशोः
सपक्ष्मा साक्षिण्यौ परिणतिरपूर्वा प्रतिदिनम्॥ ७१॥

Transliteration:
Dhanuḥ puṇyāpāṇāṁ tapam api tanoḥ pāvana-guṇaṁ
Kiyat kāraṁ yuktaṁ kimu phalam api kleśa-hataye |
Amuṣya tvannetraṁ yadu-yugalam ṛkṣaṇa-dṛśoḥ
Sa-pakṣmā sākṣiṇyau pariṇatir apūrvā pratidinam || 71 ||

Translation:
The bow of merit, austerities of the body, and purity of deeds—
how effective are they truly in ending suffering?
Each day, Your two eyes, like gentle deer,
become supreme witnesses to a new, wondrous transformation.

□

72.
Sanskrit:
अपर्णे कारुण्यं त्वयि कटाक्षावृतमनसः
अपाङ्गात्ते कुर्वन्त्यरुणधरणीमङ्गलरुचः।
दरिद्रानामिच्छान्ब्दगणनदयालोचनया
दधत्येवं मन्ये धरणिधरराजन्यतनयाम्॥ ७२॥

Transliteration:
Aparṇe kāruṇyaṁ tvayi kaṭākṣāvṛta-manasaḥ
Apāṅgāt te kurvanty aruṇa-dharaṇīm aṅgala-rucaḥ |
Daridrāṇām icchān bda-gaṇana-dayā-locanayā
Dadhaty evaṁ manye dharaṇi-dhara-rājanya-tanayām || 72 ||

Translation:
O Aparṇā, embodiment of compassion,
Your side-glances bless the earth with radiant light.
Their rosy glow seems to count the desires of the poor
with merciful eyes—revealing You as the royal daughter of Himālaya who shelters the world.

73.
Sanskrit:
समुन्नेयत्यन्तः स्फुटमपि लघुत्वेन कुरुते
गुणेनालोके ते किमपि तुलया नीलतुलया।
नीराज्यं ते दृष्टिं धिसतु निखिलं जन्मजगति
त्वदीयं सौन्दर्यं तुलयितुमहं चिन्तयति यः॥ ७३॥

Transliteration:
Samunneyaty antaḥ sphuṭam api laghutvena kurute
Guṇenāloke te kim api tulayā nīla-tulayā |
Nīrājyaṁ te dṛṣṭiṁ dhisatu nikhilaṁ janma-jagati
Tvadīyaṁ saundaryaṁ tulayitum ahaṁ cintayati yaḥ || 73 ||

Translation:
Even the manifest becomes weightless within Your inner light.
What in this world compares to the depth of Your gaze—
even the richest blue finds no match.
May all births curse the one who dares compare Your beauty.

74.
Sanskrit:

कपोलौ कालिन्दीतनुतरतरङ्गाङ्गरुचिभिः
न कुल्याभिः सिञ्चन्तौ परिषसिजतंहंसयुगलम्।
अमूनंनस्तां यं प्रसृमरशिखण्डच्छटितया
दिवं सर्वं सेन्द्रं सपदि सुवर्णैत्यभिनयेत्॥ ७४॥

Transliteration:
Kapolau kālindī-tanutara-taraṅgāṅga-rucibhiḥ
Na kulyābhiḥ siñcantau pariṣasijatāṁ haṁsa-yugalam |
Amūnāṁ nastāṁ yaṁ prasṛmara-śikhaṇḍa-cchaṭitayā
Divaṁ sarvaṁ sendraṁ sapadi suvarṇait y abhinayet || 74 ||

Translation:
Your cheeks shine like delicate waves of the Yamunā,
their glow not sprinkled by trickling streams but soaking divine swan-pairs—Your eyes.
The brilliance from Your fluttering peacock-plume beauty
instantly bathes the entire heaven, even in the presence of Indra, in golden light.

▯

75.
Sanskrit:
तव स्तोत्रं नेत्रे नयनयुगलं हन्त सकलम्
धृते स्तोत्रं योऽयं स्फुटमखिललोके विरचयेत्।
स न त्वां संस्मृत्य स्मररिपुमपि स्वान्तसुरतैः
कथं नोत्सङ्गस्थं जनयति सवित्रीव विपदम्॥ ७५॥

Transliteration:
Tava stotraṁ netre nayana-yugalaṁ hanta sakalam
Dhṛte stotraṁ yo'yaṁ sphuṭam akhila-loke viracayet |
Sa na tvāṁ saṁsmṛtya smara-ripum api svānta-surataiḥ
Kathaṁ notsaṅga-sthaṁ janayati savitrīva vipadam || 75 ||

Translation:
This hymn resides entirely within Your pair of eyes.
He who recites it with clarity across the world,
even while recalling You in his heart,

can summon Śiva, slayer of Kāma—
just as Savitrī once rescued her beloved from death.

□

76.
Sanskrit:
शरज्ज्योत्स्नाशुद्धां शशियुतजटाजूटमुकुटां
वरेण्यां भगीं त्वां वरदसुरनायिक्यमणिनाम्।
विचिन्त्येयं भक्त्या विजयति वचःपाटवमिह
न किंcit् किंcit् नो भवति गुरुतैः किम् न भवति॥ ७६॥

Transliteration:
śaraj-jyotsnā-śuddhāṁ śaśi-yuta-jaṭā-jūṭa-mukuṭāṁ
vareṇyāṁ bhagīṁ tvāṁ varada-sura-nāyikya-maṇinām |
vicintyeyaṁ bhaktyā vijayati vacaḥ-pāṭavam iha
na kiṁcit kiṁcit no bhavati gurutaiḥ kim na bhavati || 76 ||

Translation:
Like autumn moonlight—pure and serene—
You shine, O Bhagavatī, crowned with moon and divine locks.
Even the simplest speech, when offered in devotion, gains power.
And what does not become great, when inspired by You?

□

77.
Sanskrit:
कवीनां सन्दर्भस्थितमपि च सौन्दर्यलहरीं
कदा वा कारुण्यस्तुतिभिरनुचिन्त्य त्वदनघाम्।
विलोलालापानां विदधति सतां कर्णरुचिरं
न चैतत् साधूनां श्रुतिसुखमनाख्यानपदम्॥ ७७॥

Transliteration:
kavīnāṁ sandarbha-sthitam api ca saundarya-laharīṁ
kadā vā kāruṇya-srutibhir anucintya tvad-anaghām |
vilolālāpānāṁ vidadhati satāṁ karṇa-ruciraṁ
na caitat sādhūnāṁ śruti-sukham anākhyāna-padam || 77 ||

Translation:
Even poets, though skilled, rarely express
the immaculate wave of Your beauty, O Compassionate One.
Yet, Your praises—whispered with tenderness—
delight the ears of sages more than any scripture or formal speech.

▯

78.
Sanskrit:
शिवेत्येवं नाम त्रिभुवनगुरुर्गृह्णति सदा
शिवाभावेनापि स्मरति हि सदा त्वां न हि शिवः।
अतस्त्वां सम्प्रेक्ष्य प्रसृतकरगर्भामनुभवेत्
वशीकर्तुं त्वां च वशमिव जनः कामयति च॥ ७८॥

Transliteration:
śivety evaṁ nāma tribhuvana-gurur gṛhṇati sadā
śivābhāvenāpi smarati hi sadā tvāṁ na hi śivaḥ |
atas tvāṁ samprekṣya prasṛta-kara-garbhām anubhavet
vaśīkartum tvāṁ ca vaśam iva janaḥ kāmayati ca || 78 ||

Translation:
Śiva, Guru of the three worlds, always chants His name,
yet without Śakti, He is never truly Himself.
Therefore, seeing You with outstretched hands bestowing blessings,
men long to master You—
yet in truth, it is You who enchant and master them all.

▯

79.
Sanskrit:
विरिञ्चिः पञ्चत्वं व्रजति हरिराप्नोति विरतिं
विनाशं कीनाशो भजति धनदो याति निधनम्।
वितन्द्री मेत्रेयं पतति पतिरशेषगणनां
स कथं पश्यत्त्वां न पतति पयोधिं सुतनये॥ ७९॥

Transliteration:
viriñciḥ pañcatvaṁ vrajati harir āpnoti viratiṁ
vināśaṁ kīnāśo bhajati dhanado yāti nidhanaṁ |
vitandrī metreyaṁ patati patir aśeṣa-gaṇanāṁ
sa kathaṁ paśyat-tvāṁ na patati payodhiṁ sutanaye || 79 ||

Translation:
Brahmā dissolves, Viṣṇu withdraws, Yama loses his might,
Kubera dies, and the lords of all counts collapse.
O Daughter of the Ocean,
how could one see You and not be swept away like the tide?

▯

80.
Sanskrit:
त्रयीं तीर्थं वेदं सवितृमनुशास्त्राणि शिरसां
अपि ग्राम्यं काचिद्भवति हि मता तां कलितया।
अविद्या नामैनां जननिकृतमाज्ञामुपगता
महादेवीं हित्वा तव चरणसेवा न रचयेत्॥ ८०॥

Transliteration:
trayīṁ tīrthaṁ vedaṁ savitṛ-manuśāstrāṇi śirasāṁ
api grāmyaṁ kācid bhavati hi matā tāṁ kalitayā |
avidyā nām aināṁ janani-kṛtam ājñām upagatā
mahādevīṁ hitvā tava caraṇa-sevā na racayet || 80 ||

Translation:
Even those who study the Vedas, scriptures, and sacred laws
may be deemed worldly if they ignore Your splendor.
That blindness—called ignorance—is born of the Mother's will.
Forsaking You, O Great Goddess, they fail to serve at Your feet.

Verse 81

Sanskrit:
कदा काले मातः कवियशसि निःशङ्करचिता

नवोन्मेषश्रृङ्गाररससमया श्लोकमालिका ।
गुणीभूतां तावद्गुणसमुदितां गम्भीररसां
भजेन्ते सन्तः किं न तव चरणाम्भोरुहयुगम् ॥ ८१॥

Transliteration:
kadā kāle mātaḥ kavi-yaśasi niḥśaṅka-racitā
navonmeṣa-śṛṅgāra-rasa-samayā śloka-mālikā |
guṇībhūtāṁ tāvad guṇa-samuditāṁ gambhīra-rasāṁ
bhajante santaḥ kiṁ na tava caraṇāmbhoruha-yugam || 81 ||

Translation:
When, O Mother, in the fearless songs of poets,
a garland of verses is woven with new love and devotion,
rich in virtue and filled with profound meaning—
why would the wise not then worship your twin lotus feet?

□

Verse 82

Sanskrit:
स्निग्धच्छायाच्छायाच्छुरणिखरिणीशोणिमतया
दिशां सर्वासामप्यनिमिषसमीक्षाशनरुचिः ।
भवत्वन्नानाम्नां जननि नयनाम्भोरुहरुचिं
दशाश्वासद्रष्टुं दरलितदशद्रव्यरुचिरम् ॥ ८२॥

Transliteration:
snigdha-chāyā-chāyā-chchura-nikhariṇī-śoṇimatayā
diśāṁ sarvāsām apy animiṣa-samīkṣā-śana-ruciḥ |
bhavat tvannāmnām janani nayana-ambhoruha-ruciṁ
daśāśvāsa-draṣṭuṁ daralita-daśa-dravya-ruciram || 82 ||

Translation:
The red glow of your pupils, like the rays of the setting sun,
illuminates all directions with the unmoving gaze of awareness.
May the lotus eyes of your devotees, O Mother,
shine with that same light as they contemplate your form.

□

Verse 83

Sanskrit:
अवष्टम्भं भ्रान्तेः क्रियमणमिव प्रमदवतां
मनःपद्मे मध्ये सुललितरमापादि ललिताम् ।
विधत्ते सन्दर्भं कुशलविधिना काव्यसरणिं
महाशक्तिः काचित् तव करुणया मामवतु सा ॥ ८३॥

Transliteration:
avaṣṭambhaṁ bhrānteḥ kriyamaṇam iva pramadavatāṁ
manaḥ-padme madhye sulalitam apādilalitām |
vidhatte sandarbhaṁ kuśala-vidhinā kāvya-saraṇiṁ
mahā-śaktiḥ kācit tava karuṇayā mām avatu sā || 83 ||

Translation:
Like a support within illusion, in the hearts of impassioned women,
You dwell in the lotus of the mind, graceful from base to crown.
With your compassion, you weave the most refined poetry—
may that great Shakti of yours protect me.

Verse 84

Sanskrit:
तवापादद्वन्द्वं तव नयनपङ्केरुहरुचिं
सदा ध्यायन् शास्त्रं जननि तव यः स्तौति रसनाम् ।
स फण्गानां लीलां भवति बलवद्भूधरणपदां
न खल्वेष स्तोत्रं मम भवतु भूयानपि पुनः ॥ ८४॥

Transliteration:
tavāpāda-dvandvaṁ tava nayana-paṅkeruha-rucim
sadā dhyāyan śāstraṁ janani tava yaḥ stauti rasanām |
sa phaṅgānāṁ līlāṁ bhavati balavad bhū-dharaṇa-padāṁ
na khalveṣa stotraṁ mama bhavatu bhūyān api punaḥ || 84 ||

Translation:
Whoever constantly meditates on your feet and the beauty of

your lotus eyes,
and praises your glory with the Scriptures upon his tongue,
can uphold the world like the mighty serpents in play.
May this modest hymn of mine be accepted once more.

▯

Verse 85

Sanskrit:
समायाताः श्लोकाः प्रचलितकवेर्ये त्वदुदयं
विधत्ते नैवं चेत् किमपि तव सौन्दर्यलहरीम् ।
प्रबोधायासक्तं चिरमनुपमैः काव्यसरणैः
प्रणीयं त्वत्प्रेम्णा यदि न भवति स्तोत्रमथवा ॥ ८५॥

Transliteration:
samāyātāḥ ślokāḥ pracalita-kaver ye tvad-udayaṁ
vidhatte naivaṁ cet kim api tava saundarya-laharīm |
prabodhāyāsaktaṁ ciram anupamaiḥ kāvya-saraṇaiḥ
praṇīyaṁ tvat-premaṇā yadi na bhavati stotram athavā || 85 ||

Translation:
If the verses of a wandering poet do not reveal your splendor,
how can they be part of the Saundarya Lahari?
If they are not moved by love for you and longing for awakening,
then they are not hymns, but empty words.

Verse 86

Sanskrit:
त्वदन्यः पाणिभ्यां अभयवरदो दैवतः क्व न
त्वदन्यः प्रातर्नैव भवति पिताऽप्यन्यसुतयाः ।
त्वदन्यः पुण्यानामभिवननवृद्धिः फलमिति
त्वदन्यः सम्पत्तीः वितरति सदा त्वत्कृपधरः ॥ ८६॥

Transliteration:
tvadanyaḥ pāṇibhyām abhaya-varado daivataḥ kva na
tvadanyaḥ prātarnai'va bhavati pit'āpy anyasutayāḥ |
tvadanyaḥ puṇyānām abhivana-navṛddhiḥ phalam iti

tvadanyaḥ sampattīḥ vitarati sadā tvat-kṛpa-dharaḥ || 86 ||

Translation:
What other deity, but You, grants both fearlessness and boons with both hands?
What other father cares at dawn for children not his own?
Only You, O Mother, are the fruit of all virtuous acts—
Only You ever bestow blessings, full of grace.

□

Verse 87

Sanskrit:
विधेर्ज्ञानेनापि क्लिश्यति तु भवत्पादपदवीं
अनाप्त्वा सम्प्राप्तुं किल कठिनता यत्तु लभते ।
ततः किं पश्यामः स्फुरति भुवि यः पादनलिनं
भवत्या यः स्तोत्रं कथयति जनः साचि विमलः ॥ ८७॥

Transliteration:
vidher jñānenāpi kliśyati tu bhavat-pāda-padavīṁ
anāptvā samprāptuṁ kila kaṭhinatā yattu labhate |
tataḥ kiṁ paśyāmaḥ sphurati bhuvi yaḥ pāda-nalinaṁ
bhavatyā yaḥ stotraṁ kathayati janaḥ sāci vimalaḥ || 87 ||

Translation:
Even Brahmā suffers, striving with knowledge to reach your lotus feet—
but rarely does he attain them.
So who else but one who chants your hymn with a pure heart
can make your feet shine forth in this world?

□

Verse 88

Sanskrit:
गते कर्णाभ्यर्णं गमितशिरसः सप्तपदिकां
गिरं सिद्धो जानीते तव वपुषि निःशेषमहिमम् ।
पुनश्च त्वच्छेषं स्रजमपि गृह्णात्यरुणिमा

ललाटे भाति स्मेरतरलतरं माधवपतेः ॥ ८८॥

Transliteration:
gate karṇābhya-arṇaṁ gamita-śirasaḥ sapta-padikāṁ
giraṁ siddho jānīte tava vapuṣi niḥśeṣa-mahimam |
punaś ca tvac-cheṣaṁ srajam api gṛhṇāty aruṇimā
lalāṭe bhāti smerataralataraṁ mādhava-pateḥ || 88 ||

Translation:
One who attentively listens to the sevenfold hymn and bows in reverence
can truly grasp the boundless glory of your form.
Even the smile on Vishnu's radiant brow
bears the glow of your crimson garland.

Verse 89

Sanskrit:
क्व चेदं सौन्दर्यं क्व च तव गुणा क्वैव सुगतिः
क्व चैतज्ज्ञानं वा क्व च तव मनोज्ञा कृतिरियम् ।
इति चिन्ताक्रान्तं हृदयमिदमेतेन गदितं
कुविन्दः कथ्यन्ते खलु बहुलं भक्तिपरया ॥ ८९॥

Transliteration:
kva cedaṁ saundaryaṁ kva ca tava guṇā kvaiva sugatiḥ
kva caitaj-jñānaṁ vā kva ca tava manojñā kṛtir iyam |
iti cintākrāntaṁ hṛdayam idam etena gaditaṁ
kuvindaḥ kathyante khalu bahulaṁ bhakti-parayā || 89 ||

Translation:
Where does your beauty reside, and your virtues, and your divine grace?
Where is such knowledge found, and where this enchanting creation of yours?
Thus, overwhelmed by wonder, the heart proclaims:
only through deep devotion can one speak of You truly.

Verse 90

Sanskrit:
कदा काले मातः कवनपि स सन्धानविधिना
कृतश्लोकैर्युक्तं स्तवमिह सुरेन्द्रैरपि कृतम् ।
पठित्वा साम्राज्यं व्रजति पृथिवीमित्यवगता
स्मृतिर्नो चेतः स्फुरतु सुमनःसङ्गतिवशात् ॥ ९०॥

Transliteration:
kadā kāle mātaḥ kavan api sa sandhāna-vidhinā
kṛta-ślokair yuktaṁ stavam iha surendrair api kṛtam |
paṭhitvā sāmrājyaṁ vrajati pṛthivīm ity avagatā
smṛtir no cetaḥ sphuratu sumanaḥ-saṅgati-vaśāt || 90 ||

Translation:
When, O Mother, someone composes fitting verses,
an adorned hymn sung even by celestial kings,
and recites it—he attains lordship over the earth.
May this memory awaken in my mind
through the company of pure-hearted ones.

Verse 91

Sanskrit:
प्रदीपो जल्लोलिः सपदि हि निकषाय यमिनां
तवाक्ष्म्णां ब्रह्मा तृणविषयसंदर्पणचमूः ।
विधत्ते सन्धत्ते जननि मनसि त्वां गिरिसुते
विधत्ते सन्धत्ते जगति भवतीं यः स तु धन्यः ॥ ९१॥

Transliteration:
pradīpo jalloliḥ sapadi hi nikaṣāya yamināṁ
tavākṣmaṇāṁ brahmā tṛṇa-viṣaya-saṁdarpaṇa-camūḥ |
vidhatte sandhatte janani manasi tvāṁ girisute
vidhatte sandhatte jagati bhavatīṁ yaḥ sa tu dhanyaḥ || 91 ||

Translation:

The light of your gaze becomes the purifying flame for yogis.
Even Brahmā, with all his pride in worldly knowledge,
seems like a child playing with straw.
Blessed is he who holds you, O Daughter of the Mountain,
in his mind and sees You in all the world.

▯

Verse 92

Sanskrit:
अविज्ञातं तत्तत्रिभुवनवधूभङ्गरचना-
विदध्यासीत्को वा तव जननि रूपं न खलु यत् ।
नभोमध्येदूरे धरिणिधरपत्न्याः सुत इति
भवत्या एव स्वं वपुषि सख्यं नयति हि ॥ ९२॥

Transliteration:
avijñātaṁ tattvaṁ tribhuvana-vadhū-bhaṅga-racanā
vidadhyāsīt ko vā tava janani rūpaṁ na khalu yat |
nabho-madhye dūre dhariṇī-dhara-patnyāḥ suta iti
bhavatyā eva svaṁ vapuṣi sakhyaṁ nayati hi || 92 ||

Translation:
Who could fathom your true nature, O Mother,
the one behind the beauty of the maidens of all three worlds?
Though said to be the distant daughter of Himavat,
it is You yourself who manifests your own divine form.

▯

Verse 93

Sanskrit:
गिरीन्द्राणां त्वद्देहकृतधवलक्लिन्नवपुषां
सुतानामेवायं ननु तनुभवः स्तुत्यतमताम् ।
महीनां मध्यक्षं स्मरशरकलाकल्पलतिका
सकलं तत्त्वानां किमपि तुलये त्वां न जननीम् ॥ ९३॥

Transliteration:
girīndrāṇāṁ tvad-deha-kṛta-dhavala-klinna-vapuṣāṁ

sutānām evāyaṁ nanu tanubhavaḥ stutya-tamatām |
mahīnāṁ madhyakṣaṁ smara-śara-kalā-kalpa-latikā
sakalaṁ tattvānāṁ kim api tulaye tvāṁ na jananīm || 93 ||

Translation:
Among the daughters of the lords of mountains,
only You, O Mother, sanctify even Śiva's form.
You are the essence of Kāma's floral arrows,
the vine of divine desire.
How could I compare You to anything? You are beyond all.

□

Verse 94

Sanskrit:
त्वया हृतं वामं वपुर्अपरितृप्तेन मनसा
शरीरार्धं शम्भोः शकलमपरा पक्षमपि यत् ।
अपुत्रं ते पश्यन् जननि सहगर्भं तनुभुवां
इषद्वृष्ट्या पृष्टं करुणमणिना त्वं हि गिरसि ॥ ९४॥

Transliteration:
tvayā hṛtaṁ vāmaṁ vapuḥ aparitṛptena manasā
śarīrārdhaṁ śambhoḥ śakalam aparaṁ pakṣam api yat |
aputraṁ te paśyan janani saha-garbhaṁ tanu-bhuvāṁ
iṣad-vṛṣṭyā pṛṣṭaṁ karuṇa-maṇinā tvaṁ hi girasi || 94 ||

Translation:
You claimed the left half of Śiva's body,
driven by a longing mind not yet satisfied.
You completed his being with your presence.
Seeing the world as childless,
You touched it with the pearl of your compassion.

□

Verse 95

Sanskrit:
मृगाक्षीमाक्ष्मीरं स्त्रजमपि सहस्त्रैरपि करैः

गरिष्ठं ते मातः क्षणमुपगतेयं सुमनसाम् ।
समुच्चारं सान्द्रं प्रणयभरसारं कवितयाः
स्मरं स्मृत्वा स्मृत्वा बहु रतिरसार्द्रं विकसते ॥ ९५॥

Transliteration:
mṛgākṣīm ākṣmīraṁ srajam api sahasrair api karaiḥ
gariṣṭhaṁ te mātaḥ kṣaṇam upagateyaṁ sumanasām |
samuccāraṁ sāndraṁ praṇaya-bhara-sāraṁ kavitayāḥ
smaraṁ smṛtvā smṛtvā bahu ratirasārdraṁ vikasate || 95 ||

Translation:
Even with a thousand hands offering garlands and perfumes,
nothing equals a single moment
when pure hearts recall You in love.
The memory of You, steeped in poetry,
blooms with the nectar of divine passion.

▯

Verse 96

Sanskrit:
सुधामप्याशेप्यं धरणिधरकन्ये तव कृपाम्
अपीतं यैर्नैव क्शपितमवधिः त्रिभुवनम् ।
न गुण्याः केयं न खलु परिपूर्णाः पशुपतेः
कृतार्थास्ते मन्दाः कथमचरणं जानतु बुधः ॥ ९६॥

Transliteration:
sudhām apy āśepyaṁ dharaṇīdhara-kanye tava kṛpām
apītaṁ yair naiva kṣapitam avadhiḥ tribhuvanam |
na guṇyāḥ keyaṁ na khalu paripūrṇāḥ paśupateḥ
kṛtārthās te mandāḥ katham acaraṇaṁ jānatu budhaḥ || 96 ||

Translation:
Your grace, O Daughter of the Mountain,
is sweeter than nectar and inexhaustible even when drunk.
It is not due to merit, nor is Śiva himself complete without You.
How can the wise ignore your feet,
when even the dull find fulfillment through You?

▯

Verse 97

Sanskrit:
कलत्रं वैधात्रं कतिक बहव: सन्ति गहने
सरोजे क्षेत्रेऽस्मिन् श्रुतिसत्सरसीसञ्चरणधी: ।
शरीरं त्वं शंभो: शशिमिहिरवक्षोरुहयुगं
तवात्मानं मन्ये भगवति नवात्मानमहितम् ॥ ९७॥

Transliteration:
kalatraṁ vaidhātraṁ katika bahavaḥ santi gahane
saroje kṣetre'smin śruti-sat-sarasī-saṁcaraṇa-dhīḥ |
śarīraṁ tvaṁ śambhoḥ śaśi-mihira-vakṣoruha-yugaṁ
tavātmānaṁ manye bhagavati navātmānam ahitam || 97 ||

Translation:
In this lotus-field of the heart, many seek divine union.
You, who move through the sacred streams of the Vedas,
are the very body of Śiva—his sun and moon-like breasts.
I believe, O Divine One,
You are the Supreme Ninth Self beyond all.

▯

Verse 98

Sanskrit:
त्वदीयं सौन्दर्यं तुहिनगिरिकन्ये तुलयितुं
कवीनां कल्पन्ते कथमपि विरिञ्चिप्रभृतय: ।
यदालोकौत्सुक्यादमरललनायान्ति मनसा
तपोभिर्दुष्प्रापामपि गिरिशसायुज्यपदवीं ॥ ९८॥

Transliteration:
tvadīyaṁ saundaryaṁ tuhina-giri-kanye tulayituṁ
kavīnāṁ kalpante katham api viriñci-prabhṛtayaḥ |
yadālokautsukyād amara-lalanā yānti manasā
tapobhir duṣprāpām api giriśa-sāyujya-padavīm || 98 ||

Translation:
O Daughter of the Snowy Mountain,
even Brahmā and the great poets
struggle to describe your beauty.
Yearning for a glimpse of it,
celestial maidens forsake even the rare union with Śiva.

▯

Verse 99

Sanskrit:
किलाकिञ्चित्कानां कुटिलमुकुटानां चुटिकया
किरित्कोषप्रान्तस्थितकनकनिःसृष्टसिकता ।
न तृष्णा पाशत्र्यं भवति मुखत: स्फीतकटितट्य:
तव श्रीशृङ्गारे गरलमथनीव विजयते ॥ ९९॥

Transliteration:
kilākiñcitkānāṁ kuṭila-mukuṭānāṁ cuṭikayā
kirit-koṣa-prānta-sthita-kanaka-niḥsṛṣṭa-sikatā |
na tṛṣṇā-pāśa-trayaṁ bhavati mukha-taḥ sphīta-kaṭi-taṭyaḥ
tava śrī-śṛṅgāre garala-mathanīva vijayate || 99 ||

Translation:
As the curling locks of heavenly maidens loosen their jeweled crowns,
gold dust spills like sand from the rims.
From your hips to your face, the triple noose of desire dissolves—
your divine beauty triumphs, like the churner of the poison ocean.

▯

Verse 100

Sanskrit:
नितान्त: श्रोतव्यं किमपि तव तत्त्वं च भगवति
निदाने सर्वासां प्रतिफलमुपाधौ च सततम् ।
न य: शृणोत्येनं स भवति हि मुक्ता: सुकृतिभि:
तथा स्तोतुं देव्या: प्रभवति न कोऽपि त्वदन्य: ॥ १००॥

Transliteration:
nitāntaḥ śrotavyaṁ kim api tava tattvaṁ ca bhagavati
nidāne sarvāsāṁ pratiphalam upādhau ca satatam |
na yaḥ śṛṇoty enaṁ sa bhavati hi muktāḥ sukṛtibhiḥ
tathā stotuṁ devyāḥ prabhavati na ko'pi tvadanyaḥ || 100 ||

Translation:
Your essence, O Divine One, is supremely worth hearing,
the source and the fruit of all that exists.
Who does not hear this hymn cannot be freed,
and none but You can truly praise the Goddess—
for You are both the hymn and its fulfillment.

Meaning and Significance of the Saundarya Lahari

The Saundarya Lahari is not merely a devotional hymn, but a text of profound esoteric and metaphysical knowledge. Here are some of its fundamental aspects:

1. Tantric Vision of the Divine Mother
• The Goddess is not just an abstract energy, but a living and powerful presence.
• She is the creative force of the universe and the principle of spiritual transformation.

2. Mantras and Yantras
• Each verse contains powerful mantras that awaken the inner energies.
• Some verses reveal the sacred geometry of yantras—mystical diagrams for meditation.

3. The Science of Kundalini
• The text describes the awakening of kundalini, the divine energy dormant within human beings.
• The Goddess is associated with the various chakras, representing the ascent of consciousness.

□

Conclusion

The Saundarya Lahari is one of the highest and most powerful hymns dedicated to the Divine Mother. It not only glorifies the beauty of Tripura Sundarī, but also offers deep teachings on the nature of reality, consciousness, and spiritual awakening.

Reading and meditating on this hymn can lead to profound inner transformation, opening the path to the realization of the Absolute.

8. Manisha Panchakam (The Five Stanzas of Supreme Wisdom)

by Adi Shankaracharya

The Manisha Panchakam is a short yet profoundly powerful hymn composed by Adi Shankaracharya after a deep spiritual encounter. In it, the master summarizes the essence of Advaita Vedanta, declaring that whoever has realized their identity with Brahman is, regardless of their social status or physical condition, a true knower of the Self and a worthy spiritual teacher.

▯

Historical Context of the Manisha Panchakam

It is said that Adi Shankaracharya, while walking through the streets of Varanasi, encountered a man of low caste—a Chandala, considered impure by Brahmanic law. For a moment, Shankara asked the man to move aside to let him pass. The Chandala, however, posed a striking question:

"O great sage, whom are you asking to step aside?
This body, which is merely matter?
Or the Atman, which is eternal and indivisible?
If the Atman is one, how can there be purity or impurity?"

This question instantly illuminated Adi Shankaracharya's mind, and he composed the Manisha Panchakam on the spot, declaring that the true sage is not one born into a high caste, but one who has realized unity with Brahman.

▯

Text in Sanskrit, Transliteration, and Translation

▯

Verse 1

Sanskrit:
जाग्रत्स्वप्नसुषुप्तिषु स्फुटतरा या संविदुज्जृम्भते
या ब्रह्मादिपिपीलिकान्ततनुषु प्रोक्ता परा या शिवा ।
यास्वात्मन्यपि विप्रतर्पणकरी सा चेत्समस्ता मनीषा
चाण्डालोऽस्तु स तु द्विजोऽस्तु गुरु रित्येषा मनीषा मम ॥ १॥

Transliteration:
Jāgrat-svapna-suṣuptiṣu sphuṭatarā yā saṁvid-ujjṛmbhate
Yā brahmādi-pipīlikānta-tanuṣu proktā parā yā śivā |
Yā svātmany api vipratārpaṇa-karī sā cet samastā manīṣā
Cāṇḍālo’stu sa tu dvijo’stu guru rityeṣā manīṣā mama || 1 ||

Translation:
He whose consciousness shines clearly through waking, dreaming, and deep sleep,
Who perceives that same supreme awareness in both Brahmā and the tiniest ant,
Who recognizes the Self as the ultimate reality fulfilling all desires —
If such wisdom is present, then he is my Guru, whether Chandala or Brahmin. This is my firm conviction.

▯

Verse 2

Sanskrit:
ब्रह्मैवाहमिदं जगच्च सकलं चिन्मात्रविस्तारितं
सर्वं चैतदविद्यया त्रिगुणयासेषं मया कल्पितं ।

इत्थं यस्य दृढा मतीः सुगतरेः कुर्वन् पुमान् सन्ध्यति
चाण्डालोऽस्तु स तु द्विजोऽस्तु गुरु रित्येषा मनीषा मम ॥ २॥

Transliteration:
Brahmaivāham idaṁ jagac ca sakalaṁ cin-mātra-vistāritaṁ
Sarvaṁ caitad avidyayā tri-guṇayāseṣaṁ mayā kalpitaṁ |
Itthaṁ yasya dṛḍhā matīḥ su-gatareḥ kurvan pumān saṁdhyati
Cāṇḍālo'stu sa tu dvijo'stu guru rityeṣā manīṣā mama || 2 ||

Translation:
He who has realized that the entire universe is nothing but an expansion of pure consciousness,
And that all appearances are mere projections of ignorance and the three gunas—
He who walks firmly in this truth on the path to liberation—
If such wisdom is present, then he is my Guru, whether Chandala or Brahmin. This is my firm conviction.

▯

Verse 3

Sanskrit:
यतिर्वा स गृहीजनो द्विजवरों योऽप्यश्रमो वाऽपि वा
नीचो वाऽपि जडो मन्दोऽप्यथ भगवद्भक्तिमतामुत्तमः ।
यो ज्ञात्वाऽत्मानमीशं निजमनसि सदा भावयत्येव मां
चाण्डालोऽस्तु स तु द्विजोऽस्तु गुरु रित्येषा मनीषा मम ॥ ३॥

Transliteration:
Yatir vā sa gṛhī vā dvija-varo v'āpy aśramo v'āpi vā
Nīco vā yadi vā śvapāko'pi jano dṛṣṭa-parātmatām |
Sa brahmaṇy api śobhate bhuvanaṁ saṁpūrṇam etan mayā
Cāṇḍālo'stu sa tu dvijo'stu guru rityeṣā manīṣā mama || 3 ||

Translation:
Whether a renunciate or householder, a Brahmin or one without social standing,
Even if of low birth or an outcaste—
If one has seen the Supreme Self within,

He shines with Brahman and fills the whole world with its presence.
If such wisdom is present, then he is my Guru, whether Chandala or Brahmin. This is my firm conviction.

▯

Verse 4

Sanskrit:
यत्सौख्यं बुधबोधगम्यं परमं योगीश्वराद्वेष्टितं
यद्वाचाऽमनसाऽतिगं तनुभृता भृम्यत्भिरन्तर्निशम् ।
तत्स्वयं विदितं मुनीन्द्र हृदयस्थं ब्रह्मैव नैघ्ण्यं
चाण्डालोऽस्तु स तु द्विजोऽस्तु गुरु रित्येषा मनीषा मम ॥ ४॥

Transliteration:
Yat saukhyaṁ budha-bodha-gamyaṁ paramaṁ yogīśvarādveṣṭitaṁ
Yad-vāc'āmanas'ātigaṁ tanu-bhṛtā bhṛmyadbhi-rantar-niśam |
Tat svayaṁ viditaṁ munīndra hṛdaya-sthaṁ brahmaiva naiḥghnyaṁ
Cāṇḍālo'stu sa tu dvijo'stu guru rityeṣā manīṣā mama || 4 ||

Translation:
He who has known that supreme bliss
—grasped only by the wise and great yogis,
Beyond speech and mind, sought day and night by embodied beings—
He who has directly realized that Brahman dwelling in the heart—
If such wisdom is present, then he is my Guru, whether Chandala or Brahmin. This is my firm conviction.

▯

Verse 5

Sanskrit:
हेयं दुःखमिदं तथैव निजसंदोहमहंपादपीडितं
किं वा ब्रूयां यदि श्रुतिमुखैः प्रत्यग्निरन्तर्गतं ।

शुद्धं ब्रह्म विवेकदृक्प्रमथितोऽस्मीत्यविद्यायाः
चाण्डालोऽस्तु स तु द्विजोऽस्तु गुरु रित्येषा मनीषा मम ॥ ५॥

Transliteration:
Heyaṁ duḥkham idaṁ tathaiva nija-saṁdoha-mahaṁ-pāda-pīḍitaṁ
Kiṁ vā brūyāṁ yadi śruti-mukhaiḥ pratyagni-rantargataṁ |
Śuddhaṁ brahma viveka-dṛk-pramathito'smīty-avidyāyāḥ
Cāṇḍālo'stu sa tu dvijo'stu guru rityeṣā manīṣā mama || 5 ||

Translation:
He who has renounced all suffering and the burdens of ego and attachment,
Who, through the light of the Self and the guidance of the scriptures,
Has burned away ignorance with the fire of discrimination (viveka),
And abides as the pure Brahman—
If such wisdom is present, then he is my Guru, whether Chandala or Brahmin. This is my firm conviction.

Final Note

These hymns require no commentary.
They have been translated and gathered with the utmost respect for their original power.
May they resonate in the hearts of those who are ready, as they have resonated in mine.
Nothing needs to be added to the truth — it reveals itself.
Om Tat Sat.

Printed in Dunstable, United Kingdom

65637411R00087